D0083041

Psychosocial Constructs of Alcoholism and Substance Abuse

The *Advances in Alcohol & Substance Abuse* series:

Psychosocial Constructs of Alcoholism and Substance Abuse

Barry Stimmel, MD, Editor

NOV 2 1 1987

The Haworth Press
New York

＃96855 34

Psychosocial Constructs of Alcoholism and Substance Abuse has also been published as *Advances in Alcohol & Substance Abuse,* Volume 2, Number 4, Summer 1983.

Copyright © 1983 by The Haworth Press, Inc. All rights reserved. Copies of articles in this publication may be reproduced noncommercially for the purpose of educational or scientific advancement. Otherwise, no part of this work may be reproduced or utilized in any form or by any means, electronic or mechanical, including photocopying, microfilm and recording, or by any information storage and retrieval system, without permission in writing from the publisher. Printed in the United States of America.

The Haworth Press, Inc., 28 East 22 Street, New York, NY 10010

Library of Congress Cataloging in Publication Data

Main entry under title:

Psychosocial constructs of alcoholism and substance abuse.

"Has also been published as Advances in alcohol & substance abuse, volume 2, number 4, summer 1983"—T.p. verso.
Includes bibliographical references.
1. Alcoholics—Psychology—Addresses, essays, lectures. 2. Narcotic addicts—Psychology—Addresses, essays, lectures. 3. Alcoholism—Social aspects—Addresses, essays, lectures. 4. Substance abuse—Social aspects—Addresses, essays, lectures. I. Stimmel, Barry, 1939- . [DNLM: 1. Alcoholism—Psychology. 2. Substance abuse—Psychology. W1 AD432 v.2 no.4 / WM 270 P9735]
HV5045.P75   1983   362.2'9'019   83-12615
ISBN 0-86656-244-3

Psychosocial Constructs of Alcoholism and Substance Abuse

Advances in Alcohol & Substance Abuse
Volume 2, Number 4

CONTENTS

EDITOR

BARRY STIMMEL, MD, *New York, NY*

EDITORIAL BOARD

THEODORA ANDREWS, MS, *West Lafayette, IN*
MONIQUE BRAUDE, PhD, *Rockville, MD*
JOHN N. CHAPPEL, MD, *Reno, NV*
SIDNEY COHEN, MD, *Los Angeles, CA*
PAUL CUSHMAN, MD, *Richmond, VA*
VINCENT DOLE, MD, *New York, NY*
ARTHUR FALEK, PhD, *Atlanta, GA*
LORETTA P. FINNEGAN, MD, *Philadelphia, PA*
ROSS FISHMAN, PhD, *New York, NY*
MARK S. GOLD, MD, *Summit, NJ*
CHARLES W. GORODETZKY, MD, PhD, *Lexington, KY*
EULOGIO JEREZ, MD, *New York, NY*
EDWARD KAUFMAN, MD, *Orange, CA*
BENJAMIN KISSIN, MD, *Brooklyn, NY*
HERBERT D. KLEBER, MD, *New Haven, CT*
MARY JEANNE KREEK, MD, *New York, NY*
CHARLES S. LIEBER, MD, *Bronx, NY*
JACK H. MENDELSON, MD, *Belmont, MA*
ROBERT B. MILLMAN, MD, *New York, NY*
JOHN P. MORGAN, MD, *New York, NY*
S. JOSEPH MULÉ, PhD, *Brooklyn, NY*
ERNEST P. NOBEL, PhD, MD, *Los Angeles, CA*
WILLIAM POLLIN, MD, *Rockville, MD*
JANE S. PORT, *New York, NY*
S. N. PRADHAN, MD, PhD, *Washington, DC*
RICHARD B. RESNICK, MD, *New York, NY*
E. M. SELLERS, MD, PhD, *Toronto, Canada*
EDWARD C. SENAY, MD, *Chicago, IL*
HOWARD SHAFFER, PhD, *Cambridge, MA*
SPENCER SHAW, MD, *Bronx, NY*
ERIC J. SIMON, PhD, *New York, NY*
KARL VEREBEY, PhD, *Brooklyn, NY*
JOSEPH WESTERMEYER, MD, *Minneapolis, MN*
SHELDON ZIMBERG, MD, *New York, NY*
NORMAN E. ZINBERG, MD, *Cambridge, MA*

Psychosocial Constructs
of Alcoholism
and Substance Abuse

Dependency on Mood-Altering Drugs: The Need for a Holistic Approach

Why people drink excessively and/or become dependent upon other mood-altering substances has long been a subject of controversy. Is dependency a medical disorder, a manifestation of an underlying psychologic disturbance, a result of defective parenting, or merely a reaction to the adverse socioeconomic factors that confront large segments of our society?

Advocates of different points of view are often unyielding with respect to the primacy of their particular school of thought. More than two decades ago, sitting in an audience being addressed by a panel of "experts" as to the reasons why people take drugs, a curious phenomenon occurred. The panel, which consisted of a psychiatrist, a social worker, a psychologist, an internist and a former heroin addict, was running behind schedule. Four of the five members had clearly, albeit lengthily, pressed their theories concerning drug use, leaving little time for the final speaker. The moderator, undoubtedly in an attempt to put the session back on course, turned to the audience and said, "Unfortunately we have little time left, but perhaps we can hear for a few minutes from our last panelist as to why he became addicted to heroin." The gentleman rose slowly, looked at the audience, said, "It gave me great pleasure," and sat down. A woman sitting next to me responded in a muted voice, "I would have said it relieves the pain."

Unfortunately, all too many professionals in the fields of alcoholism and substance abuse tend to have a unidimensional approach,

© 1983 by The Haworth Press, Inc. All rights reserved.

absorbing from the literature, as well as their personal experience, only that information which tends to confirm their own biases. The factors leading toward alcoholism and narcotic dependency are more similar than different, yet concerned professionals in each of these fields tend to maintain their separateness rather than become competent in the management of both dependencies. While the needs of individuals may vary, as will the complications associated with the abuse of different drugs, nonetheless, the psychological and physiological factors surrounding the abuse of all mood-altering drugs are indeed quite similar, although, depending on the degree of abuse and the selection of a specific drug, differences can be discerned.

The focus of this issue of *Advances* is a review of selected psychosocial constructs dealing with alcoholism and substance abuse in an attempt to acquire a broader knowledge base to aid in both treatment and prevention. The papers selected do not provide a comprehensive view but address current areas of concern and controversy.

Individuals who drink excessively or take narcotic drugs have common, underlying personality disturbances usually characterized by a severe ego weakness, the inability to combat an intensely strong need for dependency, a low degree of tolerance for frustration and tension, and a marked ambivalence toward the parental constellation which is often a single parent family or one parent who is quite punitive and has a similar dependency. Anger is not expressed outwardly but turned within, resulting in guilt feelings manifested by self-destructive behavior.[1-5] When these factors are combined with an intense need for oral gratification, alcohol is the primary drug used to enhance one's self-esteem and, at times, to allow the person the freedom to act out those feelings unable to be expressed in the sober state. On the other hand, the presence of a greater degree of self-destructiveness, accompanied by the need to obtain relief through withdrawal and introversion, may lead to the use of heroin. The overlap between the use of these two drugs is considerable and, in fact, alcohol has been found to be the single, most frequent drug consumed by heroin addicts prior to the onset of their heroin dependency.

Advocates of the addictive personality, however, run into considerable difficulty when attempting to define whether many of the "characteristic" traits predated the development of the dependency, were a consequence of the dependency or, in fact, really differed at all from similar traits existing in a nondependent population. Midanik,[6] in this issue of *Advances,* surveys the coexistence of problem drinking and depressive symptoms in the general population. Not unexpectedly the highest rates of problem drinking occurred among those who were unemployed, single, or encountering severe environmental stresses. The lack of awareness of existing depression accompanying alcohol consumption was quite prevalent among men when compared to women. This finding is important to consider when attempting to therapeutically address alcoholism. This unawareness of coexisting psychological factors may at times make it quite difficult to engage a person in therapy or establish meaningful treatment goals other than the behavioral approach to merely cease drinking.

In contrast, women readily identified their depressive symptoms. These symptoms were highest in women who were separated, had lower incomes and lower educational levels. Midanik's findings confirm other data with respect to women and psychotropic drug use which report that women tend to take more prescribed mood-altering substances in every category of psychotropic drugs.[7] The linkage between alcoholism and depression suggests that those who drink are more likely to be taking tranquilizers and/or hypnotics and other sedatives. This not only intensifies their dependency and enhances the potential for overdose reactions but, in addition, makes it mandatory that psychologic support be provided when instituting therapy.

Lest one think that men by refusing to recognize their depressive symptoms are immune from this disorder, the study by McLellan et al[8] is pertinent. These investigators assessed the development of psychiatric disorders among men who abused stimulants, depressants (including alcohol) and opiates over a six-year time frame. At baseline examination, although all had low levels of symptomatology, no intergroup differences existed. At the end of six years, 8 of 14 (57%) depressant users had serious depression. No changes in psychopathology were noted in the opiate users, whereas 5 of 11 (45%) stimulant users had developed psychoses.

The primacy of an existing character disorder in narcotic dependency as compared to the development of a disorder secondary to use of the narcotic, however, continues to be debated. The use of an illicit substance such as heroin, unlike alcohol, is accomplished at great financial and personal cost not only to the user but to other members of society as well. The advocates of legalizing heroin claim a benefit would be reaped by both addict and society, while opponents are equally vociferous in their condemnation. Most recently, the debate has again come to the fore with three publications: one advocating a decentralized system of physician prescribed heroin;[9] one vehemently opposing heroin maintenance;[10] and the third looking hopefully toward societal trends and new pharmacological developments to alleviate the problem.[11]

Existing evidence, demonstrating that an individual becomes deviant subsequent to consuming heroin rather than developing these characteristics prior to the dependency, however, is far from compelling. Studies have demonstrated the existence of deviant behavior and illegal activities to predate the onset of narcotic use by several years.[12,13] In England, where narcotics can be obtained legally, criminal activity was noted both prior to the onset of narcotic dependency as well as subsequent to enrollment in a free clinic.[14,15]

The complexity of this problem is well described in this issue by Rounsaville et al[16] who identified two, mutually exclusive types of antisocial behavior in individuals enrolled in a large, drug-dependent unit. Approximately 27% of the population studied were considered primary antisocial addicts, demonstrating antisocial activities independent of the need to obtain drugs. An equal proportion, however, demonstrated antisocial behavior directly related to the drug use. Not surprisingly, both of these groups were distinguished from the remaining 46% of the population by having a history of heavier drug use, as well as greater criminal activity. Individuals categorized as primary antisocial were found to have greater disturbances in the family constellation, as well as more severe psychopathology, including, not unexpectedly, alcoholism. This study emphasizes the need to refrain from generalizations concerning the etiology of heroin addiction, the addictive personality, and simplified solutions to this problem, such as the legalization of heroin.

The adverse physiologic effects of alcohol and illicit narcotics on psychosocial function have been well documented. Alcohol is a toxic substance, affecting many organ systems. Heroin, while pharmacologically perhaps more benign than alcohol, nonetheless, when injected illicitly with its contaminants and adulterants, is also associated with a wide array of serious medical complications. One aspect of behavior of continuing concern is the effects of these drugs on sexual function. The literature addressing this subject is often confusing.[17,18] There is no question that experimentally both alcohol and narcotics can exert effects on the hypothalamic system, including those hormones associated with sexual function. The altered sexuality often reported accompanying their use, however, may not only have predated drug use but, in fact, feelings of sexual inadequacy may have been a contributing factor in initiation of the dependency.

The review by Price and Price,[19] therefore, concerning alcohol and sexual functioning is quite timely. These authors demonstrate that, although the biochemical effects of alcoholism are unquestioned, nonetheless, its actual effect on sexual function depends on an interplay between physiological and psychological factors, including social expectations. The variability in sexual responsiveness due to alcohol consumption is considerable. Indeed, as demonstrated by the authors, it appears that in the absence of severe, persistent alcoholism, the most important determinants of sexual functioning are the expectations of the individual user rather than the physiological effects of the drug.

Assuming that one understands the complexities involving the development of a dependency and the various treatment modalities available to individuals in need of such services, a major problem is the development of a strategy to facilitate the entry into treatment. This is obviously no small task. Of the estimated 13 million alcoholics and problem drinkers in this country, perhaps less than ten percent are in any form of therapy.[10] Of the estimated 500,000 addicts in the United States, 239,000 are believed to be in New York State, with 177,500 in New York City. Yet registries compiled by the Division of Substance Abuse Services of New York rarely list more than 35,000 in any type of therapeutic setting at any one time. This problem is perhaps most acute with adolescents who are more prone to experiment with mood-altering substances and, unfortunately, are often less likely to avail themselves of existing treatment modalities.

Dembo et al[20] review the difficulties existing in reaching youths in the inner cities. The population studied revealed 33% to have used alcohol, 90% marijuana and less than 7% hallucinogens, stimulants, depressants, mood elevators and narcotics for the past six months. Through examining various services existing for these adolescents, the authors demonstrated the need for a variety of available resources. Adolescents, at different levels of drug involvement and coming from different demographic areas, will not be attracted to the same extent to similar resources. Most important was the finding that those youths from tough neighborhoods associated with high drug use clearly identify "acceptable" and "unacceptable" services. The counselors more acceptable to these youths were peers who had overcome their personal use of drugs. Youths not involved in specific drug use or using only alcohol, on the other hand, appeared to be amenable to traditional prevention programs run by professionals or by existing services within a particular institution.

Providing acceptable treatment facilities, however, is only one step in the management of adolescent substance abuse. The marked disturbances described earlier often found in interfamily relationships mandate family involvement to insure the greatest chances for success. Friesen[21] reviews the role of the family in the initiation of substance abuse, as well as the importance of adequately exploring these relationships to determine which persons could benefit from family therapy. When disturbed family interactions are prominent, addressing these issues becomes an important part of the therapeutic endeavor.

The ability to attract adults into drug treatment programs may at times be equally difficult. The stigma attached with admitting an alcohol or drug abuse problem, combined with the demands made by these programs at a time when one's concerns are usually focused on financial support of a family, makes it quite difficult to freely engage in a therapeutic effort. Nonetheless, as demonstrated by Singh and Williams,[22] the "weariness" of drug use does show a linear relationship with age. Attempts at "deaddiction" were positively related to chronological maturation. The recognition of the need for treatment, however, was found to vary with a number of factors, including ethnicity. Blacks were more likely to seek treatment on their own than whites or Hispanics for abuse of all drugs, including alcohol. Another variable was the actual drug of abuse. Those addictions associated with the greatest degree of self-destruction, such as opiates, were associated with the largest number of people likely to seek treatment on their own. The use of substances perceived as being of relatively little harm, such as marijuana, was associated with far less frequent self-referrals. These findings confirm the hypothesis of Winick[23] and Brill[24] of a maturing out of a narcotic addiction. The subsequent course, once abstinence from narcotics has been achieved, however, is often far from satisfactory. As demonstrated by Des Jarlais et al,[25] abstinence from narcotics is often accompanied by dependence on alcohol with equal if not greater adverse consequences. This cross dependency, not infrequently observed between narcotics and alcohol, once again emphasizes the need for a concerted effort in the management of alcoholism and narcotic dependency.

The effectiveness of the available treatment modalities for alcoholism and other drugs of abuse remains of concern and has been discussed extensively in other issues of *Advances*.[26] The papers presented in this issue, however, reenforce the importance of adequately developing well-defined goals and objectives based on the characteristics of those to be served. Recognition of existing psychological and sociological milieus is equal in importance to the correction of existing physiologic abnormalities. The holistic approach to patient care is being emphasized with increasing frequency in the medical literature. Nowhere is this of greater importance than when addressing effective therapy for alcoholism and narcotic addiction.

Barry Stimmel, MD

REFERENCES

1. Blum EM. Psychoanalytic views of alcoholism: A review. Q J Studies Alcohol. 1966; 27:259-99.

2. McCord W, McCord W. Origins of alcoholism. Stanford: Stanford University Press, 1960.

3. Rado S. Narcotic bondage: a general theory of the dependence of narcotic drugs. In: Hoch PH, Zuben J, ed. Problems of addiction and habituation. New York: Grune and Stratton, 1958:27-36.

4. Savitt RA. Psychoanalytic studies on addiction: ego structure in narcotic addiction. Psychoanl Q. 1963; 32:43-57.

5. Harbin HT, Maziar HM. The families of drug abusers: a literature review. Family Process. 1975; 14:411-31.

6. Midanik L. Alcohol problems and depressive symptoms in a national survey. Advances in Alcohol & Substance Abuse. 1983; 2:9-28.

7. Parry H. The use of psychotropic drugs by U.S. adults. Public Health Service Rep. 1968; 83:799-810.

8. McLellan AT, Woody GE, O'Brien CP. Development of psychiatric illness in drug abusers. N Engl J Med. 1979; 301:1311-14.

9. Trebach AS. The heroin solution. New Haven: Yale University Press, 1982.

10. Califano JA. Drug abuse and alcoholism. New York: Warner Books, 1982.

11. Kaplan J. The hardest drug: heroin and public policy. Chicago: U Chicago Press, 1982.

12. Stimmel B. Heroin dependency: medical, social and economic aspects. New York: Stratton Intercontinental Medical Book Corp, 1975.

13. Weissman JC. Understanding the drug and crime connection. J Psychedelic Drugs. 1978; 10:171-92.

14. Mott J, Taylor M. Delinquency amongst opiate users. England: Home Office Research Studies No. 23, H.M. Stationery Office, 1974.

15. D'Orbán PT. Criminality as a prognostic factor in opiate dependence. Brit J Psychiatry. 1975; 127:86-9.

16. Rounsaville BJ, Eyre SL, Weissman MM, Kleber HD. The antisocial opiate addict. Advances in Alcohol & Substance Abuse. 1983; 2:29-42.

17. Cushman P. Neuroendocrine effects of opioids. Advances in Alcohol & Substance Abuse. 1981; 1:77-99.

18. Cicero TJ. Pathogenesis of alcohol induced endocrine abnormalities. Advances in Alcohol & Substance Abuse. 1982; 1:87-112.

19. Price JA, Price JH. Alcohol and sexual functioning - a review. Advances in Alcohol & Substance Abuse. 1983; 2:43-56.

20. Dembo R, Schmeidler J, Taylor RW, Agresti D, Burgos W. Preferred resources for help with a drug problem among youths living in different inner city neighborhood settings. Advances in Alcohol & Substance Abuse. 1983; 2:57-75.

21. Friesen VI. The family in the etiology and treatment of drug abuse: toward a balanced perspective. Advances in Alcohol & Substance Abuse. 1983; 2:77-89.

22. Singh BK, Williams JS. Chronological maturation and attempts at deaddiction: an extension of the maturation hypothesis. Advances in Alcohol & Substance Abuse. 1983; 2:91-101.

23. Winick C. The life cycle of the narcotic addict and of addiction. Bull Narc. 1964; 16:1-11.

24. Brill H. The process of deaddiction. New York: The Free Press, 1972.

25. Des Jarlais DC, Joseph H, Dole VP, Schmeidler J. Predicting post treatment narcotic use among patients terminating from methadone maintenance. Advances in Alcohol & Substance Abuse. 1982; 2:57-68.

26. Evaluation of Drug Treatment Programs. Advances in Alcohol & Substance Abuse. 1982; 2:1-117.

Alcohol Problems and Depressive Symptoms in a National Survey

Lorraine Midanik, PhD

ABSTRACT. The relationship between alcohol problems and depressive symptoms is examined in a national sample of U.S. adults (N = 1772) conducted in 1979. Although men were more likely to report alcohol problems while women were more likely to report depressive symptoms, the rates of overlap for both disorders were approximately equal for men and women when the total sample or current drinkers only are considered. However, when problem drinkers are analyzed separately, the percent of overlap for females was approximately twice that of males. Thus, these data support a growing body of clinical research which suggests that females with alcohol problems are more likely to report depressive symptomatology.

I. INTRODUCTION

Issues surrounding the relationship between alcohol and depressive symptoms are not only of current interest to researchers and clinicians in the alcohol and mental health fields, but they also have a historical significance in that they reflect how past providers of medical and psychiatric care have diagnosed and treated a variety of conditions. Early clinicians handling problems associated with melancholia, a precursor of modern-day notions of depression, did not debate specific elements of the relationship between alcohol and depressive mood, such as their time-ordering or causative natures;

Lorraine Midanik is with the Alcohol Research Group, Institute of Epidemiology and Behavioral Medicine, Medical Research Institutes, 1816 Scenic Avenue, Berkeley, California 94709.

Parts of this paper were presented at the 12th Annual Medical-Scientific Conference of the National Council on Alcoholism, American Medical Society on Alcoholism and the Research Society on Alcoholism, April, 1981. This research was supported by an Alcohol Research Center grant (AA-05595-01) from the National Institute on Alcohol Abuse and Alcoholism.

The author wishes to thank Walter Clark, Kathy Janes, Genevieve Knupfer and Raul Caetano for their comments and help on this paper.

© 1983 by The Haworth Press, Inc. All rights reserved.

9

rather, for the most part, it was assumed that melancholia was the "problem" and alcohol was often the treatment.

Examples of this phenomenon are provided by J. R. Whitwell[1] in his book on the history of psychiatry. The following passage illustrates the curative power of alcohol which includes its ability to transport the "disease" from within the body to outside the body.

> Wine, taken moderately, causeth melancholiness easily to pass through the pipes thereof, from the liver to the spleen further to the mouth of the stomach, and thus out of the body. Melancholy engendreth heaviness, faintness of heart, and covetousness, but wine engendreth joy, boldness, stoutness of stomach, and liberality. (Regimen Sanitatis Salernitanum, 1575)

While this brief quote from the 16th century does not provide a complete historical account, it does elaborate a treatment paradigm which is no longer shared by the present-day medical community. That is, alcohol is currently not the preferred treatment for symptoms of depression. We can speculate that the discovery and ubiquitous use of drugs in the 20th century, such as anti-depressants and sedatives, contributed to a new meaning of treatment to the wide range of practitioners. In addition, the rise of the alcoholism movement, beginning in the late 1930s and early 1940s, helped promote a non-psychiatric model of "alcoholism" thereby supporting either a total separation of these two "disease" entities or a conceptualization of depression as a "normal" part of alcoholism—a sequela of alcohol withdrawal.

Why, then, is there currently a concern about the relationship between depressive symptoms and alcohol use? Part of this concern is based on the expressed need of clinicians in the mental health and alcohol fields to treat all problem areas effectively when patients with alcohol problems present themselves with symptoms of depression. A second concern stems from the growing literature of "special problems of women alcoholics," i.e., affective disorders. This is evidenced by a recommendation from the proceedings of a workshop, funded by the National Institute on Alcohol Abuse and Alcoholism (NIAAA), entitled "Alcoholism and Alcohol Abuse among Women: Research Issues":

> The relationship between alcoholism and affective disorders, especially depression, should be extensively studied. An at-

tempt should be made to validate the subdivision of female alcoholics into "primary" and "affective disorder" alcoholics, and the efficacy of different treatment methods for these subgroups should be determined. The value of lithium treatment for affective disorder alcoholic women should be systematically tested and further hormonal research carried out to determine the possible value of estrogen therapy for depressed alcoholic women.[2]

The purpose of this paper is twofold. First, it will provide a description of the prevalence of alcohol problems and depressive symptoms occurring separately and conjointly in a national population survey. Second, rates of alcohol problems, depressive symptoms and their overlap will be compared with an emphasis on sex differences. Thus concerns, primarily stemming from the clinical community, about the severity of depression problems for women with alcohol problems can be assessed in this general population sample.

II. Background

Much of the alcohol research in the United States has been directed towards deriving one number which best represents the extent to which alcohol problems exist. Estimates obtained from survey data are far higher than those from clinical populations and are based, to some extent, on arbitrary criteria which can be adjusted up or down when it is convenient to do so.[3] Discrepancies between survey and clinical estimates are justified by notions of "hidden alcoholism" and "denial of alcohol problems" attributed to those in the population with, as yet, untreated alcohol problems. Room[4] has discussed in depth the history and implications of the "numbers" problem in alcohol research. He cited the research by Edwards et al.[5] as an example of a project which attempted to bridge these "two worlds" of alcohol problems. Their work in a district in London indicated that only between 10-25% of those identified as problem drinkers in a community survey were known to have actually received any alcoholism treatment services.

Alcohol problems in clinical populations are generally more severe and tightly clustered than in general population groups. Data from surveys usually indicate that alcohol problems are reported by many people but very few respond in any manner which resembles a clinical syndrome.[4,6] In addition, the clinical alcoholic population is somewhat older than those reporting alcohol problems in surveys and these problems reported in the general population at one point in time are not necessarily the same problems reported by the same people at a later point in time.[3]

One very consistent finding in the alcohol literature in both clinical and general population studies is the excess of males reporting alcohol problems. This phenomenon has been discussed extensively by Gomberg[7] in her review of alcoholism in women. She notes several explanations for these differences including Knupfer's[8] concept of "cultural protection" of women and the notion of "closet drinking" or drinking at home which is more prevalent for women.

The same issue of clinical versus general population prevalence estimates exists in the mental health field—as evidenced by the high rates of psychiatric symptoms reported by Srole and his colleagues[9] in their midtown Manhattan study. Comstock and Helsing[10] point out that rates of depression based on admission to institutions are helpful for administrative purposes but are far too limited to assess accurately the condition in a community setting. In addition, hospital cases of depression may not only be indicative of the more severe cases but may also be based more on the patient's socioeconomic status.[11]

Extensive reviews of the epidemiology of depression in both clinical and general populatons show one consistent finding, i.e., women report much higher rates of depression than men.[12,13] Explanations for these differences range from genetic/biological susceptibility to psychological and sociological factors.[14,15]

Unlike work within the field of alcohol problems and within the field of depressive symptoms, the concomitant relationship between these two areas has been studied almost exclusively on clinical populations. However, while clients in alcohol treatment facilities often report feelings of sadness or depression during and after drinking episodes, it is unclear to many clinicians how much of this unhappiness is the direct result of the pharmacologic effects of the drug, the life setting in which the clients are living and/or the disappointment of feeling unable to handle their problems with alcohol.[16] Thus, much emphasis has been placed on differentiating primary and secondary depression and alcoholism based on the time-ordering of specific life events. This nosology, proposed by Robins and Guze[17] for psychiatric diagnoses and utilized in the alcohol field by Schuckit et al.,[18] defines a primary condition as one which occurs in the absence of other disorders while a secondary condition exists in conjunction with preexisting nonaffective psychiatric disorders. This type of a schema requires extensive histories from patients with the assumption that they can accurately time-order specific life events and not restructure their past history according to providers' expectations (a major flaw of retrospective data).

Estimates of rates of depression in alcoholics generally range from 28-50 percent[19-21] with women reporting higher rates than men.[18,22] However, Pottenger et al.[23] in their study of 61 outpatients in an alcoholism treatment clinic, found that a rather high percentage of their sample (59%) were depressed, as defined by the Raskin Depression Scale, and this depression persisted by the time of follow-up one year later. They concluded that treatment strategies should include attention to depression along with the alcohol problems.

A more recent study of this overlap was reported by Woodruff et al.[24] who explored the differences among three groups of patients at a psychiatric clinic: 29 alcoholics without depression, 39 alcoholics with depression and 139 patients with depression alone. They found that alcoholics with and without depression were more alike than patients with depression only, on a variety of behavioral dimensions. They concluded that, for treatment purposes, primary alcoholics and primary depressives should continue to be separated. Schuckit,[16] referring to Winokur et al.[25] and Freed,[26] derived an estimate of the proportion within the population who are alcoholic with an affective disorder. He proposed that alcoholism and unipolar affective disorder would occur in the population at a rate of .2%-.4%; the concurrence of alcoholism and bipolar depression would be much lower (.04%).

Because the 1979 National Drinking Practices Survey is the first national study which has included both a detailed and extensive list of alcohol problem items and a reliable and valid depressive symptoms scale, we have the unique opportunity to test Schuckit's prevalence estimates. In addition, we will be able to assess differential reporting rates for males and females in the general population. Two important factors must be considered in the analysis of these survey data. First, because the survey is cross-sectional, it is impossible to time-order any events which are comparable to clinical histories. In this study, respondents were asked about their depressive symptoms *currently* and their alcohol problems within the last year. Therefore, classifications such as primary and secondary or unipolar and bipolar depressives cannot be made. Second, cutoff points on scales are somewhat arbitrary. They can be used to generate very large prevalence rates or very small ones. "Absolute" rates of any disorder in the population should be examined with extreme caution. Therefore, this paper will focus on deriving rates of alcohol problems, depressive symptoms and their overlap and will not label specific response patterns as "alcoholic" or "depressive."

III. METHODS

In 1979, a national drinking practices survey was contracted by the National Institute on Alcohol Abuse and Alcoholism with the Social Research Group of the University of California at Berkeley as part of a continuous effort on the part of the federal government to monitor alcohol use and alcohol problems in the population. A stratified area-probability sampling frame was used to draw a sample of adults 18 years or older, living within the coterminous states. Within the 2696 selected households one adult was chosen on a random basis to be interviewed. The crude response rate was approximately 69 percent, a figure based on the 1772 interviews used in analysis. While a higher response rate would have been more desirable, an analysis of the demographic characteristics and the drinking practices of the non-respondents revealed that those not included in the study were similar to the study population. In order to insure that the sample closely approximated the study population, a fairly complex weighting scheme was applied. Face-to-face interviews were of approximately one hour in length. Of the 1772 respondents in the study, approximately 66% were current drinkers, i.e., drank within the last 12 months. Most of the analysis will be confined to this subgroup.

Within the interview schedule, current drinkers were asked detailed questions on their drinking practices. For this analysis, alcohol scales were developed which measured three important domains of alcohol problems: Social Consequences of Drinking—problems with friends, relatives, spouses, jobs, and/or police/accidents associated with drinking; Loss of Control—being unable to stop drinking; and Alcohol Dependence—physiological symptoms or behaviors due to heavy consumption of alcohol or one's withdrawal from alcohol.

The alcohol field is replete with debates concerning what constitutes an alcohol problem and how it can be measured. Clark and Midanik[6] have emphasized the arbitrariness of alcohol measures. They point out that while some researchers emphasize the importance of self-reported signs of addiction, such as tremors and blackouts, as "true" indicators of dependence on alcoholism, it is unclear whether these symptoms represent long-term changes or whether they are short-term results of a heavy drinking episode. In addition, dependence symptoms are most often reported among young male drinkers in general population surveys.[27-29] Most of these individuals "mature out" by the time they reach their late twenties or early thirties. Still this contrasts with the clinical world in which dependence symptoms are tightly clustered and are most frequently found in middle-aged males.[30]

For purposes of the initial analysis in this paper, a fairly liberal definition of alcohol problems will be used. That is, "any alcohol problem" will be defined as a positive response on any of the three problem scales: Social Consequences, Alcohol Dependence or Loss of Control. Thus, we will be able to establish relatively high rates of alcohol problems which will be analyzed with depressive symptoms. More restrictive definitions of alcohol problems will also be used within the analysis (Alcohol Dependence *or* Loss of Control only; Alcohol Dependence *and* Loss of Control) for comparative purposes.

Respondents were also asked about the frequency with which specific depressive symptoms had occurred in the past week. Depressive symptoms were measured by The Center for Epidemiologic Studies Depression Scale (CES-D Scale) which was designed for use in general population surveys. It is a short, twenty-item scale comprised of questions obtained from the clinical literature and factor analytic studies. Components of the scale include: depressed mood, feelings of guilt and worthlessness, feelings of helplessness and hopelessness, psychomotor retardation, loss of appetite, and sleep disturbance.[31] Validity and reliability studies have been conducted on the CES-D scale primarily on clinical populations. The scale has been shown to have high internal consistency and moderate test/retest reliability. It has been validated against other depression scales and clinical ratings. In addition, it has been used in clinical alcohol populations and has discriminated depressed from non-depressed alcoholics when compared with ratings from physicians.[32] It cannot, however, differentiate between primary and secondary depression or unipolar and bipolar depression. The CES-D scale was included in the latter half of the interview schedule and was administered by the interviewer. Throughout the analysis a cutoff point of 16 or more on the CES-D scale was used to define depressive symptoms in the population. This has been considered to be a reasonable dividing line which differentiates clinically depressed patients from those who do not report depressive symptoms.[10,33,34]

IV. RESULTS

One way to begin to explore the relationship between alcohol problems and depressive disorders in this general population sample is to examine and compare the demographic characteristics of men and women who reported problems in either area. Table 1 presents the demographic profile of those respondents reporting any alcohol problem and of those respondents who obtained a score of 16 or more on the CES-D scale. Not surprisingly, sex differences have a strong effect on rates of problem drinking and on rates of depressive disorders. Reported rates of alcohol problems for males are twice the rate of females in the sample (21.4% and 11.5%). This relationship is reversed for males and females reporting depressive symptoms (7.2% and 16.2%). When age and sex are considered conjointly, their effect varies. Alcohol problems seem to be very strongly linked to age for both sexes. Younger age groups, particularly 18-25 year olds, had the highest rates of alcohol problems with men having consistently higher rates than women. Although women report higher rates of depressive symptoms than men in each age category, no consistent trend emerged for age and depressive disorders. However, women who are 66 years of age and older reported lower rates of depressive symptoms than the younger aged women.

Within the mental health field, marital status has been considered an important variable in relation to risk of specific disorders. These data support the notion that marriage has somewhat of a protective effect for men in relation to alcohol problems. Only 14.8% of the married men in this sample reported any alcohol problem in the last year as compared to 32.6% of the divorced men, 42.8% of the separated men, 28% of the widowed men and 33.7% of the never married men. Married women shared a lower rate of alcohol problems with women who are divorced or separated; however, never

Table 1

Demographic Characteristics of Current Drinkers[1]
Reporting Any Alcohol Problem[2] in the Last 12 Months
or Depressive Symptoms[3]
(in percents[4])

	Any Alcohol Problem		Depressive Symptoms		TOTAL N
	%	(N)	%	(N)	
TOTAL	16.7	(197)	11.5	(144)	1169
Sex					
Male	21.4	(127)	7.2	(39)	562
Female	11.5	(70)	16.2	(105)	607
Age					
Males					
18-25	35.5	(43)	11.3	(10)	109
26-35	28.9	(38)	5.8	(8)	135
36-45	15.8	(16)	7.4	(7)	89
46-55	9.9	(14)	3.0	(4)	94
56-65	9.5	(9)	5.5	(5)	73
66+	11.3	(7)	9.0	(5)	61
Females					
18-25	20.7	(31)	16.7	(27)	148
26-35	11.8	(20)	16.7	(28)	164
36-45	11.6	(11)	22.8	(25)	110
46-55	10.1	(7)	13.6	(12)	77
56-65	2.0	(1)	16.6	(7)	53
66+	-	(0)	6.6	(6)	54
Marital Status					
Males					
Married	14.8	(59)	4.9	(19)	356
Divorced	32.6	(14)	6.2	(2)	47
Separated	42.8	(7)	12.8	(2)	14
Widowed	28.0	(3)	3.0	(1)	19
Never been Married	33.7	(44)	13.4	(15)	126
Females					
Married	9.4	(31)	13.7	(46)	346
Divorced	12.4	(12)	19.7	(20)	77
Separated	8.4	(1)	47.4	(8)	21
Widowed	-	(0)	12.2	(8)	51
Never been Married	23.3	(26)	20.2	(23)	111

1. Respondents who reported drinking within the last 12 months.
2. A positive reponse to any of three alcohol problems scales: Social Consequences, Alcohol Dependence, Loss of Control.
3. Score of 16 or more on the CES-D scale.
4. Percents are weighted figures; totals shown are the actual number of cases.

Table 1 (continued)

	Any Alcohol Problem		Depressive Symptoms		TOTAL N
	%	(N)	%	(N)	
Total Income Before Taxes					
Male					
Under $4,000	33.9	(8)	23.4	(5)	20
$4,000-9,999	28.2	(24)	9.0	(6)	95
$10,000-19,999	24.5	(48)	5.6	(12)	183
$20,000-29,999	18.7	(22)	6.9	(8)	104
$30,000-39,999	12.7	(9)	3.3	(2)	67
$40,000 and over	15.9	(10)	9.5	(4)	58
Female					
Under $4,000	22.6	(8)	32.9	(13)	35
$4,000-9,999	13.2	(16)	23.7	(28)	124
$10,000-19,999	9.8	(19)	12.6	(25)	173
$20,000-29,999	9.9	(9)	15.9	(19)	117
$30,000-39,999	12.5	(4)	11.0	(4)	41
$40,000 and over	18.2	(7)	9.9	(5)	46
Education					
Male					
Less than 7 years	18.1	(4)	19.2	(4)	22
7-11 years	22.4	(33)	9.0	(12)	133
12 years	23.1	(42)	8.4	(13)	168
Some college	26.6	(27)	4.6	(5)	105
Graduated from college	12.4	(8)	3.0	(3)	58
Post grad. work	12.8	(10)	3.0	(2)	67
Female					
Less than 7 years	61.7	(4)	89.3	(6)	7
7-11 years	9.7	(15)	27.7	(37)	120
12 years	11.4	(23)	10.5	(24)	222
Some college	12.7	(17)	15.6	(25)	143
Graduated from college	4.1	(3)	9.4	(6)	65
Post grad. work	14.3	(41)	8.0	(4)	41
Ethnic Background					
Male					
White	19.6	(101)	6.3	(31)	472
Black	22.1	(11)	12.7	(4)	49
Hispanic	62.7	(10)	11.1	(2)	19
Other	23.8	(4)	10.7	(1)	17
Female					
White	10.7	(52)	14.6	(78)	514
Black	10.6	(7)	21.6	(13)	55
Hispanic	25.8	(7)	32.1	(9)	23
Other	25.5	(4)	29.9	(4)	13

Table 1 (continued)

	Any Alcohol Problem		Depressive Symptoms		TOTAL N
Employment Status	%	(N)	%	(N)	
Male					
Employed	21.8	(99)	6.5	(26)	431
Unemployed	45.9	(11)	14.0	(3)	22
Student	12.1	(3)	-	(0)	15
Homemaker	-	(0)	-	(0)	0
Retired	9.2	(8)	10.3	(8)	77
Disabled	42.4	(6)	18.1	(2)	15
Female					
Employed	12.7	(43)	15.9	(55)	353
Unemployed	20.6	(9)	26.8	(14)	38
Student	33.0	(4)	36.8	(5)	14
Homemaker	9.0	(14)	12.9	(20)	147
Retired	-	(0)	12.3	(8)	49
Disabled	-	(0)	25.8	(3)	5

married women reported rates approximately twice that of the other groups. When rates of depressive symptoms are considered, a different pattern emerges among men and women. Although women overall reported higher rates of depression than men in all marital status categories, women who are separated have the highest rates of depressive disorder (47.4%) whereas married women have a much lower rate (13.7%) which is similar to the rates of widowed women (12.2%). For men, the rates of depressive disorder are elevated slightly for separated and never married men, however the numbers are so small that interpretations should be made with caution.

A fairly consistent negative relationship exists between income, alcohol problems and depressive symptoms for both men and women. This pattern is similar when education is considered for females only. Education does not seem to be related to alcohol problems for men in this sample; however, males with less than a 7th grade education reported the higher rates of depressive symptoms (19.1%).

Ethnic background seems to have an effect on reports of alcohol problems among the sample population. Male Hispanics had the highest rates of alcohol problems (62.7%). Among the females, Hispanics and "Others" shared higher rates than whites and blacks in the sample. It must be noted that only 19 Hispanic males and 23 Hispanic females are included in the sample. In general, ethnic background does not seem to be related to depressive symptoms except that whites reported somewhat lower rates than blacks, Hispanics and others for both sexes.

The effect of employment status seems to be most evident in relation to alcohol problems reported by men. Unemployed and disabled men reported the highest rates of problems with alcohol (45.9% and 42.4% respectively)—rates far greater than employed males (21.8%). This was somewhat the case for females. Unemployed women had rates of alcohol problems higher than employed females (20.6% and 12.7%); however, women students reported the highest rate (33%). Generally, this pattern was repeated for depressive symptoms with employed men and women having generally lower rates than unemployed and disabled people.

In summary, the demographic characteristics of respondents reporting alcohol problems and reporting depressive symptoms are generally consistent with previous research. Alcohol problems were shown to be more prevalent among young males. Specifically, higher rates of problems with alcohol were found for males who were not married, of Hispanic background, unemployed or disabled. Youth was also associated with alcohol problems for females, as well as being single and having a lower educational level. Higher rates of depression were found for females for almost every category of demographic variable. Depressive symptoms were also more prevalent for both males and females with lower incomes and lower education levels. Females who are separated had elevated rates of depressive disorders.

Further analyses were done to examine the interplay of specific alcohol problem scales and depressive symptoms for both sexes. Table 2 presents the Pearson product-moment correlation coefficients between the alcohol problem scales and depressive symptoms for males and females. Two features of these correlation coefficients should be noted. First, although all the correlations are significant, they are quite modest—ranging between .15 to .26. Second, the association between alcohol problems and depressive symptoms is similar for both sexes. This implies that the occurrence of one type of problem with the other is not necessarily sex-specific in this sample.

This pattern is further evidenced when the degree of overlap is examined (Table 3). Note the somewhat similar percents of both males and females reporting any alcohol problem and depressive symptoms (3.6% and 3.8% respectively). However, these percen-

Table 2

Correlations of CES-D Scale with Alcohol Problem Scales,[1]
for Current Drinkers[2] by Sex

	Males	Females	Total
Social Consequences	.23	.21	.15
Alcohol Dependence	.26	.25	.21
Loss of Control	.22	.15	.15
Any Alcohol Problem[3]	.25	.21	.18

All correlations were significant at p < .05.

1. Full scale scores were used; problem scales were based on last 12 months.
2. Respondents who reported drinking in last 12 months.
3. A positive response on any of the three alcohol problems scales: Social Consequences, Alcohol Dependence, Loss of Control.

Table 3

Current Drinkers[1] Reporting Any Alcohol Problem[2],
Depressive Symptoms[3] And Both By Sex
(in percents[4])

	Males (N=562)		Females (N=607)		TOTAL (N=1169)	
	%	(n)	%	(n)	%	(n)
Any Alcohol Problem	21.4	(127)	11.5	(70)	16.7	(197)
Depressive Symptoms	7.2	(39)	16.2	(105)	11.5	(144)
Any Alcohol Problem AND Depressive Symptoms	3.6	(19)	3.8	(25)	3.7	(44)

1. Respondents who reported drinking within the last 12 months.
2. A positive reponse to any of three alcohol problems scales: Social Consequences, Alcohol Dependence, Loss of Control.
3. Score of 16 or more on the CES-D scale.
4. Percents are weighted figures; totals shown are the actual number of cases.

tages change dramatically as the denominator changes. When the degree of overlap is taken as a percent of those reporting alcohol problems (N = 127 for males; N = 70 for females), approximately one-third of the problem drinking women also reported depressive symptoms (25/70) while far fewer men had both types of problems (16.8%; 19/127).

As the definition of an alcohol problem becomes more rèstrictive, the degree of overlap can be further examined (Table 4). When alcohol problems are defined as reports of alcohol dependency *or* loss of control, rates of overlap for male and female current drinkers remain approximately the same as before for both sexes— 3.6% of the men reported both disorders; 3.8% of the women. When the denominator is "problem drinkers," the degree of overlap for this group also parallels that of the "any alcohol problem" definition—17.4% (18/116) of the male problem drinkers reported depressive symptoms; 33.1% (22/63) of the female problem drinkers. (Note that the percents are weighted.) However, when the definition of alcohol problem is further restricted to include only reports of alcohol dependency *and* loss of control, the percent of overlap decreases for male and female current drinkers (1.3% and 1.2%), yet rates of overlap increase substantially for problem drinking

Table 4

Current Drinkers[1] Reporting Alcohol Problems
(Dependence or Loss of Control; Dependence and Loss of Control)
and Depressive Symptoms[2] by Sex
(in percents[3])

	Males (N=562)		Females (N=607)		TOTAL (N=1169)	
	%	(n)	%	(n)	%	(n)
Dependence or Loss of Control	19.4	(116)	10.4	(63)	15.1	(179)
(With Depressive Symptoms)	3.4	(18)	3.4	(22)	3.4	(40)
Dependence and Loss of Control	6.6	(42)	2.3	(14)	4.5	(56)
(With Depressive Symptoms)	1.3	(9)	1.2	(8)	1.2	(17)

1. Respondents who reported drinking within the last 12 months.
2. Score of 16 or more on the CES-D scale.
3. Percents are weighted figures; totals shown are the actual number of cases.

women (56.7%; 8/14) but remain fairly constant for problem drinking men (19.0%; 9/42). This dramatic increase for women suggests that women with more severe alcohol problems are the most likely to also manifest depressive symptoms.

Table 5 presents the demographic characteristics for the male and female current drinkers who reported any alcohol problems and depressive symptoms. A comparison of these data with the characteristics of respondents who reported any alcohol problem or depressive symptoms (Table 1) reveals that the groups are similar with respect to age and marital status. That is, younger men and women and unmarried men tend to have higher rates of each and both problem types. However, this "overlap" group tends to have a higher income level and a higher educational level than the "pure" alcohol problem and the "pure" depressive symptoms groups. And, while employment status does not seem to impact on these problem rates for women, employed men have higher "overlap" rates than unemployed men.

The data that have just been presented provide an opportunity to compare the findings of this study with Schuckit's[16] population estimates discussed earlier. Schuckit proposed that 5-6% of the population have alcoholism, 4% have unipolar depression and 1-2% have bipolar depression. Based on these rates, he further derived the rates of overlap between these problem areas to be .2-.4% for unipolar depression and .04% for bipolar depression. The rates derived from the 1979 National Drinking Practices Survey differ somewhat from those proposed by Schuckit (Table 6). Note that when a very liberal definition of alcohol problem is used (any alcohol problem), the rate for the total population is quite high (11.2%). Even when this definition is restricted somewhat (alcohol dependence *or* loss of control), the rate remains fairly high (10.2%). It is only when alcohol problems are defined as alcohol dependence *and* loss of control that the rates approximate that of Schuckit's (3.1%). As discussed earlier, rates of unipolar and bipolar depression cannot be estimated in the 1979 survey by the CES-D scale. However, even if we assume that both types of depression are mutually exclusive and add the percents which were derived by Schuckit, we still do not come close to the proportion of respondents in the 1979 sample who obtained a score of 16 or more on the CES-D scale (13.9%). Finally, as expected, the rates of overlap of alcohol problems and depressive symptoms differ. Approximately 2.5% of the respondents in the national survey reported both depressive symptoms and any alcohol problem; 2.3% reported depressive symptoms and alcohol dependence *or* loss of control. Even the most restrictive definition (alcohol dependence *and* loss of control) yielded higher rates than Schuckit's estimates (.83%).

V. DISCUSSION

The data from the 1979 National Drinking Practices Survey has provided the opportunity to describe and assess the prevalence of depressive symptoms and alcohol problems occurring separately and simultaneously in a national sample. The findings suggest that

Table 5

Demographic Characteristics of Current Drinkers[1]
Reporting Any Alcohol Problem[2] and Depressive Symptoms[3] by Sex
(in percents[4])

	Males (N=19)		Females (N=25)	
	%	(n)	%	(n)
Age				
18-35	79.7	(13)	55.2	(16)
36-55	4.3	(2)	40.2	(8)
56+	15.9	(4)	6.0	(1)
Marital Status				
Married	15.9	(3)	49.3	(10)
Not Married	84.1	(16)	50.7	(15)
Income				
Under $4,000	17.4	(4)	3.0	(2)
$4,000-$9,999	31.9	(4)	44.8	(9)
Over $10,000	50.7	(9)	52.2	(12)
Education				
Less than 7 years	7.2	(1)	20.9	(4)
7-11 years	18.8	(5)	35.8	(9)
12 or more	74.0	(13)	43.3	(12)
Ethnic Background				
White	62.3	(13)	64.2	(14)
Non-white	37.7	(5)	35.8	(11)
Employment				
Employed	65.2	(12)	47.8	(13)
Non-employed	34.8	(7)	52.2	(12)

1. Respondents who reported drinking within the last 12 months.
2. A positive reponse to any of three alcohol problems scales: Social Consequences, Alcohol Dependence, Loss of Control.
3. Score of 16 or more on the CES-D scale.
4. Percents are weighted figures; totals shown are the actual number of cases.

Table 6

Comparison of Estimates of Alcoholism,
Depression and the Overlap

	SCHUCKIT (1979)	1979 NATIONAL DRINKING PRACTICES SURVEY (N=1772)		
"ALCOHOLISM"	5–6%	ANY ALCOHOL PROBLEM	11.2%[1]	(197)
		ALCOHOL DEPENDENCE OR LOSS OF CONTROL	10.2%	(179)
		ALCOHOL DEPENDENCE AND LOSS OF CONTROL	3.1%	(65)
"DEPRESSION"				
Unipolar	4%	16 or more on the CES–D Scale	13.9%	(267)
Bipolar	1–2%			
"OVERLAP"				
Unipolar	.2–.4%	16 or more on the CES–D Scale +		
Bipolar	.04%	ANY ALCOHOL PROBLEM	2.5%	(44)
		ALCOHOL DEPENDENCE OR LOSS OF CONTROL	2.3%	(40)
		ALCOHOL DEPENDENCE AND LOSS OF CONROL	.8%	(17)

[1]Percents for the 1979 Drinking Practices Survey are weighted figures; totals shown are the actual number of cases.

the relationship between these two conditions is not very strong for males or females and that the percent of overlap ranges from 1.2-3.8% for current drinkers and .8-2.5% for the total population. More importantly, the more stringent the criteria for defining problem drinking, the more likely that a female problem drinker will also report depressive symptoms (34-57%). The overlap for males, however, remained the same (17-19%). It is interesting to note that the demographic characteristics of this "overlap" group do differ from that of the "alcohol problem" group and "depressive symptoms'' group in that they tend to be employed with higher educational and income levels.

This paper has served to describe the prevalence of two disorders in a national population. One problem area, alcohol problems, is considered to be a "man's" problem with few women scoring high enough on alcohol problem scales to "qualify" as having an alcohol problem. The other area, depressive symptoms, appears to be the domain of women with relatively few men scoring high enough on the CES-D scale to be considered "depressed." Hence we have two sex-specific areas which, to some extent, cancel out in the analysis. One approach for future studies may be to consider the conceptual issues surrounding both the alcohol and depression fields. This somewhat parallels the social model of depression proposed by Brown and Harris[35] in which *meanings* of life events as they relate to depression are explored as opposed to just whether or not they occurred. What may mean depression to males may be a much lower score on the CES-D scale. Perhaps any positive response on the depression scale by men is an admission of a mood disorder of the same magnitude for women who score much higher. Alternatively, it may be that alcohol problem scores can be adjusted for women so that we are measuring the relative impact of specific consequences of alcohol use equally for men and women. The feasibility of this approach and its potential biases and limitations need to be further examined but it appears to be an intriguing research endeavor which may aid clinicians and researchers to better understand the relationship between these two, somewhat diffuse, areas.

REFERENCES

1. Whitwell JR: Historical notes on psychiatry. London: HK Lewis & Co. Ltd., 1936.

2. U.S. Department of Health, Education & Welfare: Alcohol and Women. Research Monograph No. 1, Public Health Service, 1980.

3. Clark W: Operational definitions of drinking problems and associated prevalence rates. Quart J Stud Alc. 1966; 37:1256-90.

4. Room R: Treatment-seeking populations and larger realities. In: Edwards G, Grant M, eds. Alcoholism treatment in transition. London: Croom Helm, 1980:205-24.

5. Edwards G, Hawker A, Hensman C, et al.: Alcoholics known or unknown to agencies. Brit J Psychiatry. 1973; 123:169-83.

6. Clark WB, Midanik L: Alcohol use and alcohol problems among U.S. adults: results of the 1979 national survey. Chapter 1, Alcohol and Health Monograph No. 1, Alcohol Consumption and Related Problems, NIAAA, DHHS Pub. No (AGM) 82-1190, Washington, D.C.: Supt. of Docs. U.S. Govt. Print. Off., 1980.

7. Gomberg E: Alcoholism in women. In: Kissin B. Begleiter H, eds. The biology of alcoholism, volume 4, social aspects of alcoholism. New York: Plenum Press, 1976:117-66.

8. Knupfer G: Female drinking patterns, in Selected Papers Presented at the Fifteenth Annual Meeting of the North American Association of Alcoholism Programs, Washington, D.C., 1964, pp. 140-160.

9. Srole L, Langner TS, Michael ST, Opler MKN, Rennie TAC: Mental health in the metropolis: the mid-town manhattan study. Volume 1. New York: McGraw Hill, 1962.

10. Comstock G, Helsing K: Symptoms of depression in two communities. Psych Med. 1976; 6:551-63.

11. Cooper B: Psychiatric disorder in hospital and general practice. Social Psychiatry. 1966; 1:7-10.

12. Silverman C: The epidemiology of depression. Baltimore: Johns Hopkins Press, 1968.

13. Weissman M, Klerman G: Epidemiology of mental disorders. Arch Gen Psychiatry. 1978; 35:705-12.

14. Akiskal HS, McKinney, Jr WT: Overview of recent research in depression. Arch Gen Psychiatry. 1975; 32:285-305.

15. Blaney PH: Contemporary theories of depression: critique and comparison. J Abnormal Psych. 1977; 86:203-23.

16. Schuckit MA: Alcoholism and affective disorder: diagnostic confusion. In: Goodwin D, Erickson C, eds. Alcoholism and affective disorders: clinical, genetic and biochemical studies. New York: SP Medical & Scientific Books, 1979:9-20.

17. Robins E, Guze S: Classifications of affective disorders: the primary-secondary, the endogenous and the neurotic-psychotic concepts. In: Robins E, Guze S, eds. Recent advances in psychobiology of the depressive illness. Washington, DC: DHEW Publication, U.S. Govt Printing Office, 1972.

18. Schuckit M, Pitts FN, Reich T, et al.: Alcoholism I: Two types of alcoholism in women. Arch Gen Psychiatry. 1969; 20:301-6.

19. Winokur G: Family history studies. VIII. Secondary depression is alive and well, and.... Dis Nerv System. 1972; 33:94-99.

20. Cadoret R, Winokur G: Depression in alcoholism. Ann NY Acad Sci. 1972; 233: 34-39.

21. Guze SF, Woodruff RA, Clayton PF: 'Secondary' affective disorder: a study of 95 cases. Psych Med. 1971; 1:426-28.

22. Schuckit M, Winokur G: A short-term followup of women alcoholics. Dis Nerv System. 1971; 33:672-78.

23. Pottenger N, McKernon J, Patrie L, et al.: The frequency and persistence of depressive symptoms in the alcohol abuser. J Nerv Mental Dis 1978; 166:562-70.

24. Woodruff RA, Guze S, Clayton P, et al.: Alcoholism and depression. In: Goodwin D, Erickson C, eds. Alcoholism and affective disorders: clinical, genetic and biochemical studies. New York: SP Medical & Scientific Books, 1979:49-56.

25. Winokur G, Clayton PJ, Reich T: Manic Depressive Illness. St. Louis: CV Mosby, 1969.

26. Freed EX: Alcoholism and manic-depressive disorders. Quart J Stud Alc. 1970; 31: 62-89.

27. Cahalan D: Problem Drinkers. San Francisco: Jossey-Bass, 1970.

28. Cahalan D, Room R: Problem Drinking Among American Men. New Brunswick, NJ, Rutgers Center of Alcohol Studies, Monograph No. 7, 1974.

29. Polich JM, Orvis BR: Alcohol Problems: Patterns and Prevalence in the U.S. Air Force. Santa Monica, CA: Rand Corporation, 1980.

30. Room R: Measurement and distribution of drinking patterns and problems in general populations. In: Edwards G, Gross N, Keller N, Moser J, Room R, eds. Alcohol-related disabilities. Geneva: World Health Organization, 1977:61-87.

31. Radloff L: The CES-D scale: A self-report depression scale for research in the general population. Applied Psych Measurement, 1977; 1:385-401.

32. Weissman M, Sholomskas D, Pottenger M, et al.: Assessing depressive symptoms in five psychiatric populations: a validation study. Amer J Epidemiology. 1977; 106:203-14.

33. Craig TJ, Van Natta P: Validation of the community mental health assessment inter-view instrument among psychiatric inpatients. Working paper No. B-27A for the Center for Epidemiologic Studies, 1973.

34. Weissman M, Locke B: Comparison of a self-report symptom rating scale (CES-D) with standardized depression rating scales in psychiatric populations. Presented at the 8th Annual Meeting of the Society for Epidemiological Research, Albany, NY, 1975.

35. Brown GW, Harris T: Social Origins of Depression: A Study of Psychiatric Disorder in Women. New York: The Free Press, 1978.

The Antisocial Opiate Addict

Bruce J. Rounsaville, MD
Stephen L. Eyre, BA
Myrna M. Weissman, PhD
Herbert D. Kleber, MD

ABSTRACT. Opiate addicts have frequently been characterized as having antisocial personality disorder, but rates of this diagnosis using specified diagnostic criteria have not been determined. In this paper, rates of antisocial personality disorder derived from two different diagnostic systems are reported on a sample of treated opiate addicts. Two mutually exclusive types of antisocial addicts are identified: (a) primary antisocial addicts, comprising 27.2% of the sample and consisting of those with a history of antisocial activities that are independent of the need to obtain drugs, and (b) secondary antisocial addicts, comprising 27.7% of the sample, whose antisocial behavior was found to be directly related to drug use. Both types of antisocial addicts were distinguished from those without this disorder by having a history of heavier drug use and greater evidence of criminal activity. However, the primary antisocial addicts were distinguished from both secondary antisocial addicts and non-antisocial addicts by having greater evidence of childhood disruptions and more severe psychopathology, with high rates of depression, borderline personality, and alcoholism.

Opiate addiction is frequently associated with criminal activity and possession and use of heroin is, itself, a crime. Regarding the individuals who are addicted to illicit opiates, the MMPI literature

Bruce J. Rounsaville is Assistant Professor of Psychiatry, Yale School of Medicine; Director of Research, Substance Abuse Treatment Unit, Connecticut Mental Health Center. Stephen L. Eyre is Research Associate, Substance Abuse Treatment Unit, Connecticut Mental Health Center. Myrna M. Weissman is Professor, Departments of Psychiatry and Epidemiology, Yale School of Medicine; Director, Depression Research Unit, Connecticut Mental Health Center. Herbert D. Kleber is Professor of Psychiatry, Yale School of Medicine; Director, Substance Abuse Treatment Unit, Connecticut Mental Health Center. Send reprint requests to: Bruce J. Rounsaville, MD, CMHC, 100 Park St., New Haven, CT 06511.

The research for this paper was supported by Contract #271-77-3410 from the National Institute on Drug Abuse.

© 1983 by The Haworth Press, Inc. All rights reserved.

indicates that a large number of them display an antisocial personality profile characterized by elevated scores on the Psychopathic deviance (Pd) and the Mania (Ma) scales.[1] However, the meaning of the association of antisocial behavior and personality traits with compulsive opiate use is controversial. Some investigators emphasize the criminal nature of addiction and the fact that many addicts began criminal behavior prior to becoming addicted to opiates.[2,3,4] According to this view, these individuals are likely to be exposed to opiates as a result of their prior involvement with criminals. Moreover, they are likely to have antisocial personality traits which would lead them to be attracted to opiate addiction because opiates appeal to their desire for immediate gratification, and provide the opportunity to act out manipulative tendencies through involvement with the drug world, with its drug dealing, promise of easy money, and criminal activity. An alternate view is that most opiate addicts engage in antisocial activities and adopt antisocial personality traits as a result of becoming involved with the drug dealing, manipulation of others, and commission of lucrative crimes that are necessitated by the need to avoid intolerable withdrawal symptoms.[5,6] Initial drug use may be motivated by the need to self-medicate underlying psychopathology such as depression, anxiety or severe personality disorders[7,8,9] or simply by curiosity or the desire to comply with peer pressure. However, once initial phases of intermittent, experimental use are passed and a physical dependence occurs, the dynamics of drug addiction are created primarily due to the characteristics of the drug itself and not by underlying, predisposing personality traits that are antisocial per se.[8,10-12]

An additional issue regarding antisocial personality characteristics in opiate addicts is the clinical nature of addicts with this personality type. The classic view of antisocial personalities is that they engage in exploitative behavior that violates the rights of others while experiencing little in the way of painful affects such as anxiety and depression.[13] Although the exploitive behaviors may be motivated by underlying, profound feelings of inadequacy, worthlessness, and emptiness, these feelings are rather successfully defended against.[14] On the other hand, Valliant has argued that "antisocial" opiate addicts do not fit this picture but, instead, are troubled by comparatively accessible painful affects such as anxiety and depression.[15] Moreover, the MMPI findings regarding opiate addicts should be assessed in light of the findings of Astin[16] who factor analyzed the Pd scale of the MMPI and identified five factors: (1) self-esteem; (2) hypersensitivity; (3) social maladjustment; (4) emotional deprivation; and (5) impulse control. Many of the items contained in the self-esteem, hypersensitivity and emotional deprivation groupings are highly suggestive of depression. Thus, many addicts who score as antisocial on the MMPI may have been responding primarily to the items suggesting depression, a syndrome that has been shown to be highly common in this group.[17-19] An important issue regarding the diagnosis of antisocial personality in addicts is the extent to which this subgroup can become involved in treatment due to the motivation provided by painful effects.

In this report we will evaluate the prevalence and clinical features associated with antisocial personality in opiate addicts. The data derive from a survey of psychiatric disorders in treated opiate addicts, in which we found, as reported elsewhere, that the most commonly made secondary diagnoses were major depressive disorder, alcoholism, and antisocial personality.[18] We will focus on two issues: (1) the extent to which antisocial personality traits seen in addicts are associated with or independent of drug use. To evaluate this issue we will compare rates of antisocial personality disorder diagnosed using a system that excludes drug related antisocial behavior from the inclusion criteria with rates derived from a system that includes drug associated antisocial behavior as evidence for the disorder, and (2) the clinical characteristics that distinguish addicts with the antisocial personality from those without the disorder. In particular, the extent to which antisocial manifest painful affects will be addressed.

METHODS

Setting and Sample

Subjects were evaluated at the Yale University Drug Dependence Unit of the Connecticut Mental Health Center in New Haven, Connecticut, which serves an urban and suburban population of approximately 400,000 people. This unit provides a wide variety of treatments available to clients whose primary drug of abuse is not alcohol.

Psychiatric diagnosis was obtained on 533 subjects who were contacted in the following manner:

1. A pilot sample of 157 subjects (149 of whom were evaluated using the RDC) was evaluated at the Screening and Evaluation Section, and represents a group that was seen as they were applying for treatment. One hundred seven of these 157 subjects were evaluated on a catch-as-catch-can basis and the remaining 50 subjects were consecutive admissions to treatment.
2. A sample of 204 additional consecutive admissions at the Screening and Evaluation Unit were interviewed following the completion of the pilot sample.
3. One hundred twenty subjects were members of the Methadone Maintenance program who were evaluated at least three months after being taken into the program. Sampling in this treatment program was on a catch-as-catch-can basis.
4. Sixty subjects were Hispanics who were evaluated in Spanish and were evaluated on application to treatment (n = 30) or after entering a residential therapeutic community for Hispanic patients (n = 30).

Subjects in all populations surveyed were paid for participating in the study and were interviewed only after informed written consent was obtained. For this study, opiate addiction was defined according to Research Diagnostic Criteria[20] which are as follows: withdrawal as shown by four or more of the following symptoms appearing within 24 hours of cessation of the drug: insomnia, sweating, flushing, runny nose, chills, stomach cramps, diarrhea, muscle pain, nausea, gooseflesh, or twitching; or daily or near daily use of illicit narcotics for more than two weeks; or participation in a methadone program for three weeks or more; or use of illicit narcotics three or more days per week for more than a month. The sample is described in more detail elsewhere.[4]

Assessments

Psychiatric Diagnosis. Information for making diagnostic judgements was collected on the Schedule for Affective Disorders and Schizophrenia-Lifetime Version (SADS-L).[21] On the basis of the information collected on the SADS-L, the subjects were classified on the Research Diagnostic Criteria (RDC) which are a set of operational diagnostic definitions with specific inclusion and exclusion criteria for a variety of nosologic groups.[20]

Diagnoses on the RDC are made both for the current time period (point prevalence rates) and for a lifetime (lifetime prevalence).

Other Assessments. Alcohol problems were evaluated with the Michigan Alcohol Screening Test.[22] Additional personality diagnoses were made using the Axis II criteria from the American Psychiatric Association's DSM III.[23] The Michigan Alcohol Screening Test and the DSM III personality diagnoses data were not gathered on the pilot sample.

Interviewers

There were five raters with Masters' and Bachelor-level education and previous experience in clinical psychiatry and interviewing. Under the supervision of a psychiatrist, the raters received three months of training with the SADS and RDC and other ratings. Reliability of diagnostic ratings was very good with Kappa coefficient ranging from .72-1.0 in different categories. Reliability data is reported in detail elsewhere.[24]

RESULTS

Rates of Antisocial Personality Disorder by Two Diagnostic Schemes

In a large subsample of this survey (n = 382, pilot sample excluded), the diagnosis of antisocial personality was made according to two diagnostic systems: Research Diagnostic Criteria and DSM III criteria. The two systems are highly similar in that both require that (a) the disorder be characterized by an onset of antisocial activity before age 15 and that (b) there is substantial evidence for the continuation of antisocial activities of various kinds following the age of 15. There are two key differences between the diagnostic systems. First, in the RDC, raters are instructed, in individuals with a drug use disorder to "count only those manifestations of antisocial personality which cannot be clearly attributed to the alcohol or drug problem"[20] while for the DSM III, "in the case of individuals with a drug use disorder both Substance Use Disorder and Antisocial Personality Disorder should be diagnosed if the criteria for each disorder are met, regardless of the extent to which some of the antisocial behavior may be a consequence of the Substance Use Disorder."[23] Second, for the RDC diagnosis one of the required criteria is "some evidence of markedly *impaired* capacity to sustain lasting close, warm, and responsible relationships with family, friends, or sexual partners." This aspect of behavior is included in one of the diagnostic criteria for the DSM-III but is not necessary to make the diagnosis.

In our study, it was the impression of the interviewers, who made both DSM-III and RDC ratings, that the key differentiating factor between the two systems was the RDC requirement that adult antisocial activity be independent of drug use. To evaluate this issue, we determined the number of addicts who were excluded from the diagnosis by failing to meet each of four, sequentially ordered criteria. These data are presented in Table 1. As shown there, over half of the sample had childhood antisocial activity and evidence of poor occupational functioning in adulthood. However, 21.4% were excluded from receiving the diagnosis by failing to meet criterion 3, which is non-drug related antisocial activities such as arrests, defaulting on debts, etc. Comparatively few (5.7%) addicts were excluded from the diagnosis because of failure to meet criterion 4 with impaired interpersonal functioning. Hence this latter difference between the RDC and DSM III criteria was found to have a comparatively minor impact on the rates of disorders using the two systems. By exclusion, the other major difference, that between drug related and non-drug related adult antisocial behavior, was felt to be the key differentiating factor between the two systems.

TABLE 1

ADDICTS MEETING RDC CRITERIA FOR ANTISOCIAL PERSONALITY

(n = 533)

Criterion 1 - Poor adult occupational performance

Criterion 2 - Childhood antisocial activities

Criterion 3 - Adult antisocial activities

Criterion 4 - Impaired interpersonal relationships

Number of addicts meeting criteria		Percent excluded by failure to meet criteria
1	69.6%	30.4%
1+2	53.5%	16.1%
1+2+3	32.1%	21.4%
1+2+3+4	26.5%	5.6%

If the rates of antisocial personality diagnosed according to RDC criteria are indicative of the extent to which addicts manifest this personality disorder independent of drug use, while the rates according to DSM III criteria indicate the presence of antisocial characteristics regardless of drug related activities, we can, by comparing the two rates, make an estimate of the extent to which two kinds of antisocial addicts exist: (a) those whose antisocial personality traits are primary and independent of drug use (Primary Antisocial Addicts); and (b) those whose antisocial personality characteristics are related to their addiction (Secondary Antisocial Addicts). If the rates using the two systems are similar, then it might be expected that most addict sociopaths are primarily sociopaths, and secondarily addicts. However, if a much higher rate of the disorder is found using DSM III criteria, then the Group meeting DSM III criteria and not RDC criteria probably represent a secondary sociopathic group whose antisocial activity has been caused, at least in part, by opiate addiction. Making this comparison, we found that the rates of antisocial personality disorder in addicts is much higher (54%) when the DSM-III criteria are used than when RDC criteria are used (27%). In that the RDC criteria appear to be more stringent, nearly all (96%) of the addicts meeting these criteria meet DSM III criteria while only around half (44%) of those meeting DSM III criteria also meet RDC criteria. Following the reasoning above, we would estimate that addicts with antisocial personality disorders fall into two roughly equal groups: (a) Primary Antisocial Addicts 27.2% of the sample; and (b) Secondary Antisocial Addicts 27.7% of the sample.

Comparison of Clinical Features in Opiate Addicts by Diagnosis of Antisocial Personality

To evaluate the clinical significance of antisocial personality in opiate addicts three groups were compared: (a) Primary Antisocial Addicts (those who met RDC criteria for the disorder); (b) Secondary Antisocial Addicts (those who met DSM III but not RDC criteria for the disorder); and (c) those who were not diagnosed as antisocial using either diagnostic system (Non-Antisocial Addicts). Inter-group differences in demographic characteristics, childhood history, legal and drug history, associated psychiatric disorders, psychological symptoms, and social functioning were assessed.

Demographic Characteristics. The sample as a whole was predominantly male (76%), nonwhite (62%), in Hollingshead and Redlich's lower social classes (81%), unmarried (66%), with a high school education or less (81%), young (mean age = 27.2), and employed full time (56%). All antisocial addicts are more likely than others to be male and in a lower social class. Regarding educational level and usual employment pattern, the Primary Antisocial Addicts have poorer achievement than Secondary Antisocial Addicts, while Non-Antisocial Addicts have the highest achievement in both areas.

Childhood History

As shown in Table 2, the three groups differ significantly in several areas of childhood history including history before age 15 of severe family disruption, severe financial difficulties, leaving home

TABLE 2

CHILDHOOD HISTORY AND PARENTAL MENTAL ILLNESS IN
OPIATE ADDICTS BY DIAGNOSIS OF ANTISOCIAL PERSONALITY

| Childhood Events Before Age 15 | Antisocial Personality | | | |
	Primary RDC Only n=104 %	Secondary DSM III Only n=106 %	No Diagnosis n=172 %	Significance of Chi² Tests
Permanent Separation (mother)	13	13	20	
Permanent Separation (father)	5	3	5	
Time in Foster Home	5	1	4	
Parental Separation	34	35	33	
Severe Family Disruption	53	31	26	****
Severe Financial Problems	30	27	17	*
Parental Physical Abuse	24	16	16	*
Left Home Permanently	18	10	7	*
First Psychiatric Treatment	10	11	4	*
School Failure	40	30	16	****
Appeared in Juvenile Court	49	43	15	****
Parental Mental Illness				
Depression	22	17	17	
Alcoholism	18	9	11	
Suicide	3	4	0	*
Any Mental Disorder	36	22	24	*

Significance Levels
   * p < .05
   **** p < .0001

permanently, receiving first psychiatric treatment, failing at least one grade at school, and appearing in juvenile court. In all cases the antisocial addicts were more likely than the Non-Antisocial Addicts to report these events and there was usually a linear relationship with Primary Antisocial Addicts having the highest rate of events than Secondary Antisocial Addicts having the next highest rate and the Non-Diagnosis Group having the lower rate. A similar pattern was noted for parental suicide while Primary Antisocial Addicts were more likely than those in the other two groups to report that a parent had some psychiatric disorder.

Legal and Drug Abuse History

In most areas of legal and drug use history listed in Table 3 addicts with antisocial personality diagnosis reported heavier drug use and arrest records than Non-Antisocial Addicts. Again a linear trend was noted in most areas in which the Primary Antisocial group had the heaviest drug and arrest record followed by the Secondary Antisocial Addict and the Non-Antisocial Addicts in that order. In several areas including alcohol problems, severity of opiate use, and total arrests, the Primary Antisocial group had records that significantly exceeded the other two groups.

Psychiatric Disorders. In addition to antisocial personality the Primary Antisocial Addicts also had the highest rate of borderline type personality disorders, the highest lifetime rate of RDC dysphoric disorders and alcoholism, and the highest current rate of alcoholism and anxiety disorders. The Non-Antisocial group had the highest rate of other personality disorders and was highly similar to the Secondary Antisocial group in rates of other disorders. See Table 4.

COMMENT

Primary and Secondary Antisocial Opiate Addicts

The rates of antisocial personality diagnosed by either system far exceed those reported from a community survey conducted in the same city in which 1% met Research Diagnostic Criteria for the disorder.[25] Although the RDC and DSM III diagnoses are based on antisocial acts and disrupted interpersonal relations in contrast to personality scales, the findings are consistent with literature based on the Minnesota Multiphasic Personality Inventory which indicates that a profile characterized by elevated Pd and Ma scales is common in opiate addicts.[1] Antisocial personality is not universal in opiate addicts as around half did not meet the less stringent DSM III criteria for the disorder and around three-fourths did not meet RDC criteria.

The difference in rates of antisocial personality was strikingly different when RDC and DSM III criteria were used. We suggest that the key difference in the two systems for this diagnosis is in the RDC requirement that adult antisocial activity be independent of the need to obtain drugs. We propose that addicts who met these criteria represent a primary antisocial group whose drug use may be secondary to exposure to criminals and to their desire to engage in the

TABLE 3

LEGAL AND DRUG USE HISTORY OF OPIATE ADDICTS BY DIAGNOSIS OF
ANTISOCIAL PERSONALITY

	Primary	Secondary		
	RDC Only n=104 mean	DSM-III Only n=106 mean	No Diagnosis n=172 mean	Significance of F-Tests
Drug Use History				
Number of previous drug treatments	2.8	2.7	2.2	
MAST score-alcohol problems	8.4	3.5	3.4	****
Age first heroin use	18.0	18.0	19.2	*
Magnitude opiate abuse (product of years of use x 7 pt. scale of severity of use)	50.1	42.1	41.0	*
Number of categories of illicit drugs used daily for at least 3 months	2.7	2.7	2.3	****
Legal History				
Number of arrests				
Crimes against persons	1.0	.4	.4	**
Property crimes	2.6	1.3	.4	***
Drug crimes	1.9	1.8	1.7	
Other crimes (e.g. prostitution or severe traffic violation)	8.2	6.4	4.1	**
Total arrests	14.9	10.3	6.9	****
Convictions	9.6	7.4	4.7	**
Number of days in past 30 engaged in illegal activities for profit	11.8	14.9	7.4	****

*=p < .05
**=p < .01
***=p < .001
****=p < .0001

Table 4

PSYCHIATRIC DISORDERS IN OPIATE ADDICTS BY DIAGNOSIS OF ANTISOCIAL

PERSONALITY DISORDER

	Antisocial Personality			
	Primary RDC Only N=104 %	Secondary DSM III Only N=106 %	No Diagnosis N=172 %	Significance of Chi^2 Tests
DSM III Personality Disorders				
Borderline group (schizotypal borderline schizoid paranoid)	28	11	8	****
Narcissistic group (dependent narcissistic histrionic)	8	9	11	
Other (avoidant passive aggressive atypical)	3	1	14	****
RDC Lifetime Disorders				
Dysphoric Disorders (major depression minor depression intermittent depression labile personality cyclothymic personality)	88	73	70	**
Manic Disorders (mania hypomania)	11	6	6	
Anxiety Disorders (panic phobic generalized obsessive compulsive)	22	18	14	
Schizophrenic Disorders	0	3	5	
Alcoholism	58	29	26	****
Current RDC Disorders				
Alcoholism	28	11	11	***
Manic or hypomanic	2	1	1	
Major or minor depression	33	28	27	
Anxiety disorder (phobic generalized panic obsessive compulsive)	19	13	7	*

Significance or Difference Levels

**** p < .0001
*** p < .001
** p < .01
* p < .05

"hustle" involved in the drug world. In contrast we suggest that the group who meet DSM III criteria but not RDC criteria have Secondary Antisocial personality traits which are derived from the need for drugs. The comparison of the clinical characteristics associated with these two diagnoses is consistent with the view that Primary Antisocial Addicts represent a generally more psychologically disturbed group with more evidence of early life disruptions than Secondary Antisocial Addicts. These two types of antisocial addicts may also be different in treatment response with Secondary Antisocial being more likely to reduce criminal activity when need for drugs is removed. The Primary Antisocial Addicts may continue to engage in criminal activities even when substitute opiates are provided. Although some studies have shown that crime rates in opiate addicts are reduced when they are maintained on opiates,[2,3] others show that criminal activity is far from eliminated when the need to obtain drugs is removed.[4,26] The Primary Antisocial addict may be responsible for the continued criminal behavior observed in these studies.

Clinical Features Associated with Antisocial Personality

Although the clinical features associated with a diagnosis of antisocial personality were frequently similar in the Primary and Secondary Antisocial Addicts, the Primary (RDC) Antisocial Addicts represented the group most distinguished from Non-Antisocial Addicts. Many of the clinical features associated with the antisocial personality diagnosis are logical extensions of the concept of antisocial personality disorder. For example, antisocial addicts could be expected to have poorer educational achievement and occupational functioning because these are included in the criteria for the disorder. Similarly a heavier arrest record and having more severe legal problems is consistent with the expected profile of an antisocial addict. However several other features associated with the diagnosis are not intuitively obvious. First antisocial addicts reported more disruptive childhood events and more parental psychopathology than non-antisocial addicts. This finding may have some significance regarding psychological development in this group as antisocial addicts might be hypothesized to have never been able to form adequate relationships with disturbed parental figures in a disrupted family environment. Alternatively the finding might support a genetic hypothesis linking antisocial personality in addicts to other categories of psychopathology in first degree relatives. Second, the association of antisocial personality with several other categories of psychiatric disorders as well as indices of neuroticism, psychological problems and psychological symptoms contradicts the picture of the typical antisocial individual as being comparatively tough-skinned and unable to experience meaningful affect. Rather, compared with non-antisocial addicts the antisocial addicts are more prone to borderline personality disorders, depressive disorders, and anxiety disorders. Thus they are a group with more severe problems with impulse control that is coupled with more severe difficulties with regulation of mood and affect as well. Going along with the more severe problems with behavior control, antisocial addicts are also more likely to have alcohol-related problems and to have poorer social functioning. This profile of antisocial addicts as having more difficulties in a broad range of areas suggests that the attempt to avoid dysphoric affect through antisocial behavior is unsuccessful.

Given the clinical profile of antisocial opiate addicts indicating a generally greater degree of disturbance in a range of areas, it might be expected that this group may be especially difficult to engage in treatment. However, in a follow-up study in which a sample of addicts were retested 6 months after applying for treatment we found that addicts with an RDC diagnosis of antisocial personality were functioning comparably with those without the disorder in the areas of occupational functioning, psychological symptoms, program retention, and illicit drug use although they were more likely to have developed further legal problems following entrance to treatment.[27] Hence, although the antisocial addict is likely to have a wider range of problems than his non-antisocial counterpart, the comparative ability to use a drug treatment program is compromised only in the area of continued illicit activity. Thus, the routine use of a complex diagnostic system to label antisocial behavior in the context of clinical programs may be less useful than evaluating legal history with specific attention to the use of illegal means to obtain financial support. This feature of the addict's current functioning has been shown by McLellan et al[28] to be of great prognostic significance in treated substance abusers.

REFERENCES

1. Craig RJ. Personality characteristics of heroin addicts: A review of the empirical literature with critique - Part II. Int J Addict 1979; 14:607-626.

2. Johnson LK, O'Malley PM, Eveland LK. Drugs and delinquency: A search for causal connections. In: Kandel DB, ed. Longitudinal research on drug abuse: Empirical findings and methodological issues. Washington, D.C.: Hemisphere Publishing Company, 1978.

3. Kandel DB. Convergences in prospective longitudinal surveys of drug use in normal populations. In: Kandel DB, ed. Longitudinal research on drug use: Empirical findings and methodological issues. Washington, D.C.: Hemisphere Publishing Company, 1978.

4. Lukoff IF. Issues in the evaluation of heroin addiction. In: Josephson E, Carroll EE, eds. Drug use: Epidemiological and sociological approaches. New York: Wiley, 1974.

5. Dupont RL. Heroin addiction treatment and crime reduction. Am J Psychiat 1972; 128:90.

6. Joseph H, Dole VP. Methadone patients on probation and parole. FED Probation 1970; 34:42.

7. Khantzian EJ, Mack JE, Schztzberg AF. Heroin use as an attempt to cope: Clinical observations. Am J Psychiat 1974; 131:160-164.

8. Wikler A. Dynamics of drug dependence: Implications of a conditioning theory for research and treatment. Arch Gen Psychiat 1973; 38:611-616.

9. Wurmser L. The hidden dimension: Psychodynamics in compulsive drug use. New York: Aronson, 1978.

10. Bejerot N. Addiction: An artificially induced drive. Springfield, Illinois: Charles C. Thomas, 1972.

11. Dole VP, Nyswander ME. Addiction—A metabolic disease. Arch Internal Med 1967; 120:19-24.

12. Zinberg NE. Addiction and ego function. Psychoanal Study Child 1975; 30: 567-588.

13. Cleckley HM. Mask of sanity. St. Louis, Missouri: C. V. Mosby Co., 1941.

14. Bursten B. The manipulator: A psychoanalytic view. New Haven, Connecticut: Yale University Press, 1973.

15. Valliant GE. Sociopathy as a human process. Arch Gen Psychiat 1975; 32:178-183.

16. Astin AW. A factor study of the MMPI psychopathic deviate scale. J Consult Psychol 1959; 23:550-554.

17. Rounsaville BJ, Weissman MM, Crits-Christoph K, Wilber CH, Kleber HD. Diagnosis and symptoms of depression in opiate addicts: Course and relationship to treatment outcome. Arch Gen Psychiat 1982; 39:151-156.

18. Rounsaville BJ, Weissman MM, Wilber CH, Kleber HD. Heterogeneity of psychiatric diagnosis in treated opiate addicts. Arch Gen Psychiat 1982; 39:161-166.

19. Weissman MM, Slobetz F, Prusoff B, Mesritz M, Howard P. Clinical depression among narcotic addicts maintained on methadone in the community. Am J Psychiat 1976; 133:1434-1438.

20. Spitzer RL, Endicott J, Robins E. Research diagnostic criteria: Rationale and reliability. Arch Gen Psychiat 1978; 35:773.

21. Endicott J, Spitzer RL. A diagnostic interview: The schedule for affective disorders and schizophrenia. Arch Gen Psychiat 1978; 37:837.

22. Selzer ML. The Michigan alcohol screening test: The quest for a new diagnostic instrument. Am J Psychiat 1971; 127:88-94.

23. American Psychiatric Association. DSM III: Diagnostic and statistical manual, Ed.3. Washington, D.C.: American Psychiatric Association, 1980.

24. Rounsaville BJ, Cacciola J, Weissman MM, Kleber HD. Diagnostic concordance in a follow-up study of opiate addicts. J Psychiat Res 1981; 16:191-201.

25. Weissman MM, Myers JK, Harding PS. Psychiatric disorders in a United States urban community: 1975-1976. Am J Psychiat 1978; 135:459-462.

26. Hawks D. The epidemiology of narcotic addiction in the United Kingdom. In: Josephson E, Carroll EE, eds. Drug use: Epidemiological and sociological approaches. New York: Wiley, 1974.

27. Rounsaville BJ, Tierney T, Crits-Christoph K, Weissman MM, Kleber HD. Predictors of treatment outcome in opiate addicts: Evidence for the multidimensionality of addict's problems. Comprehen Psychiat 1982; 23:462-478.

28. McLellan AT, Ball JC, Rosen L, O'Brien CP. Pretreatment source of income and response to methadone treatment. Am J Psychiat 1981; 138:785-789.

Alcohol and Sexual Functioning: A Review

Joy A. Price, PhD
James H. Price, PhD, MPH

ABSTRACT. The physiological and biochemical effects of alcoholism in men can lead to decreased levels of testosterone and increased levels of estrogens. This alteration in the testosterone-estrogen ratio can lead to feminization and sexual dysfunction. Research on the effects of alcoholism in women is less definitive; but nonetheless, points to alterations in sexual functioning as well.

For the non-alcoholic, acute intoxication leads to a complex interplay of physiological, psychological and social expectations which make it difficult to predict the effect of alcohol on sexual behavior. The general concensus of the experimental evidence on alcohol's impact on sexual behavior is that it is a depressant even at low concentrations. Although sexual responsiveness is often attributed to the influence of alcohol (disinhibition theory), it appears the circumstances under which it is consumed, and the psychological state of the consumer, is as important a determinant of sexual behavior.

INTRODUCTION

An awareness that alcohol alters sexual behavior was noted, at least as early as Shakespeare, in this reply to MacDuff's inquiry about the major effects of alcohol on human behavior. *Macbeth,* Act II, Scene 3: "(Drink) sir, it provokes, and unprovokes: it provokes the desire, but it takes away the performance." In contrast, alcohol's effect on women's sexuality is portrayed in such lore as "Candy is dandy; but liquor is quicker." Whether there is any biochemical or physiological basis to these widespread assumptions concerning alcohol and human sexual behavior will be the topic of this article.

The vast majority of research on sex and alcohol has dealt with impotence and signs of feminization in males. This is understand-

Joy A. Price is a medical student at the Medical College of Ohio, Toledo, Ohio. James H. Price is Professor and Chairman, Department of Health Education, The University of Toledo, Toledo, Ohio 43606. Address reprint requests to James H. Price.

© 1983 by The Haworth Press, Inc. All rights reserved.

able in terms of methods of evaluating male sexual performance and the cultural importance of sexual behavior imposed on men. However, this type of approach contributes to the denial of the significance of sexuality and sexual arousal in women. In reality the greatest adverse effect of mixing alcohol and sex lies with the woman alcoholic. Fetal alcohol syndrome is due to her overindulgence, although there is evidence that more spontaneous abortions occur in offspring fathered by alcoholic men.[1] Even if the alcoholic woman abstains from drinking alcohol prior to and during her pregnancy; previous damage to her reproductive system may adversely affect the fetus.[2] Alcohol may directly damage the gametes in both males and females but such damage would have a more lasting effect in the female since her supply of gametes does not turn over as in the male. In any case research on alcohol's impact on sexual and gonadal function in the female is scant.

BIOLOGICAL EFFECTS ON MALES

Abnormal sexual changes in male alcoholics which may be present clinically (even in the absence of liver disease) are: hypogonadism as indicated by reduced beard growth; loss of libido and impotency; testicular atrophy and reduced fertility; hyperestrogenism, indicated by gynecomastia; vascular spiders and changes in body hair and fat distribution.[3] Testicular atrophy, gynecomastic changes in body hair, and vascular abnormalities associated with alcoholic cirrhosis, have long been known and referred to as "Laennec's cirrhosis" (French physician, 1781-1826). Laennec's cirrhosis was attributed to a secondary metabolic imbalance, whereas a similar clinical presentation without accompanying liver disease was identified in the mid-1920s and called Silvestrini-Corda Syndrome. This syndrome was thought to be due to a direct toxic effect of alcohol on the testes.[4]

TESTOSTERONE LEVELS

A general concensus exists among researchers that testosterone levels in males (human and rats) are negatively correlated with alcohol consumption.[6-17] A summary of possible sites of inhibition of testosterone metabolism are shown in Figure 1 and include: a

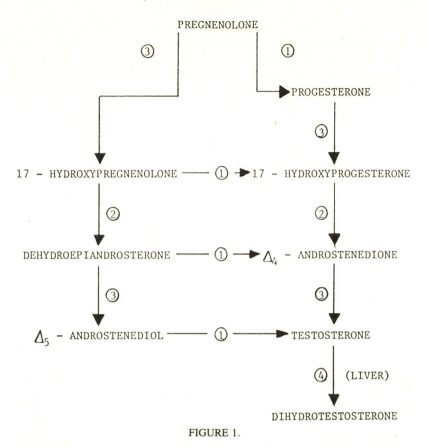

FIGURE 1.

direct effect of alcohol on the testes ① ; a direct effect of alcohol on the hypothalamic-pituitary axis ② ; changes in peripheral testosterone metabolism ③ ; changes in circulating levels of sex-hormone-binding globulin (SHBG) ④ ; increased plasma estrogen levels; and changes in estrogen receptors ⑤ .[3]

Ellingboe and Varanelli, 1976,[6] studied the effect of ethanol on testosterone production *in vivo* using sexually mature male rats and *in vitro* using isolated Leydig cells (rat). Testosterone production was stimulated via human choriogonadotropin or dibutyryl cyclic AMP. At alcohol levels of 0.1 mg/ml the percent testosterone in Leydig cells was 60 percent of controls. Levels of 10 mg/ml alcohol lowered testosterone to less than 10 percent of control levels; however, concentrations less than 0.01 mg/ml appeared to stimulate testosterone production slightly (10 percent). Blood alcohol levels of 1.7 mg/ml in the rats in the *in vivo* studies resulted in plasma testosterone levels of only 35 percent of that of controls. It should be noted that most abstainers and moderate drinkers are intoxicated at blood alcohol levels between 1.5 and 2 mg/ml. The researchers postulated that the loss of NAD in the presence of ethanol was the rate-limiting factor in testosterone decreases. They found that when they added NAD to the Leydig cells in the presence of alcohol, testosterone levels were returned to control values except at the extremely high concentrations of ethanol (10 mg/ml). The authors propose that acute alcohol reduction of testosterone levels is due to a direct effect on the testis via a shift in the NAD/NADH ratio.

Badr et al., 1977,[18] had proposed that acetaldehyde was the direct inhibitor of testosterone production in the testis, but Ellingboe and Varanelli claimed this was unlikely because acetaldehyde does not accumulate in the testis to any significant degree since testes have more acetaldehyde dehydrogenase than alcohol dehydrogenase activity. In contrast, Cicero et al., 1979,[9] argued that acetaldehyde is the more direct inhibitor of testicular steroidogenesis because inhibitors of alcohol dehydrogenase did not enhance the effect of alcohol on testosterone levels *in vivo* (rats) whereas acetaldehyde dehydrogenase inhibitors markedly increased the potency of alcohol. They proposed that ethanol by virtue of its conversion to acetaldehyde, as such, is a more potent inhibitor of testicular steroidogenesis.

TESTICULAR TOXIN

Alcohol has been shown to be a testicular toxin.[8] Van Thiel et al., 1975,[8] fed rats a diet with alcohol as 36 percent of the total calories. The rats developed significant testicular, prostatic and seminal vesicle atrophy and had greatly reduced plasma testosterone levels (less than 20 percent of controls).

HYPOTHALAMIC-PITUITARY-GONADAL AXIS

Effects of alcohol on the hypothalamic-pituitary-luteinizing hormone axis was examined by Cicero et al., 1979.[9] After an acute injection of alcohol (2.5 g/kg) in male rats, the percent decrease in serum luteinizing hormone (LH) levels were greater than the decrease in serum testosterone levels (at least for the first 60 minutes). Normally after castration of rats they show an increase in serum LH levels. Cicero demonstrated that ethanol blocked this increase in LH levels and that the effect of ethanol could be reversed by administering luteinizing hormone-releasing factor (LH-RF). This indicated that ethanol was acting at the level of the hypothalamus (lowering LH-RF) rather than at the level of the pituitary (from which LH is released). Under normal conditions testosterone served as a feedback inhibitor of LH secretion and therefore you would expect its concentration to be high under low testosterone levels. Mendelson et al., 1977,[10] reported elevated LH levels in normal human males after acute alcohol intoxication (blood alcohol levels 1 mg/ml). The fact that LH levels have been reported[11,12] within normal or low ranges, even though testosterone levels were low, can be explained by alcohol directly inhibiting hypothalamic function.

TESTOSTERONE METABOLISM

In normal males 95 percent of circulating testosterone is produced in the testes.[3] The remainder is produced in the adrenal cortex or converted from precursors, mainly androstenedione, peripherally in the liver, adipose, and neural tissues (Figures 1 and 2). Rubin et al., 1976,[13] found that in rats, after long-term alcohol ingestion, the enzymatic activity of microsomal 5-testosterone reductase had doubled, and that in human volunteers the activity had increased two to five times. This enzyme reduces the A-ring in testosterone and is the rate-limiting enzyme for metabolism of testosterone in the liver. Since the reductase is dependent upon NADPH for its activity, and ethanol causes a build-up of reducing power in the liver; alcohol consumption can increase liver clearance of metabolically active testosterone.

Gordon et al., 1980,[14] measured the activity of 3B-dehydrogenase activity and 17-hydroxylase activity of gonadal homogenates of rats fed alcohol for 40 days. They found a decrease in the activity of 3B-dehydrogenase which is dependent on NAD and/or NADP, whereas there was an increase in 17-hydroxylase activity which requires reduced co-factors (NADH and NADPH). The conversion of prognenolone to progesterone is also rate-limiting in testosterone synthesis and dependent on NAD.

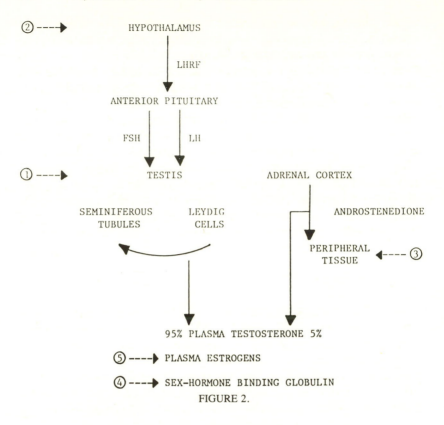

FIGURE 2.

TESTICULAR VITAMIN A METABOLISM

The imbalance in NAD/NADH levels in the testes can also cause an impairment in vitamin A metabolism which is necessary for spermatogenesis. In the testes both vitamin A and ethanol are oxidized by the same enzyme, alcohol dehydrogenase,[20] except the Km for retinol is much lower (50 times lower) than the Km for ethanol. Under normal conditions retinol is oxidized to retinal but in the presence of excess alcohol, retinal formation in testes is inhibited and aspermatogenesis may result.[20]

HYPERESTROGENISM

Normally males contain all 3 estrogens in their plasma: estrone, estradiol, and estriol. Ludholm et al., 1978,[21] found that 50 percent of the chronic alcoholics studied had increased concentrations of estradiol, but no relation could be demonstrated between the increase in estrogens and hypogonadism.

In order to explain the increased levels of estrogens in chronic alcoholics, Eagon et al., 1980,[22] examined the estrogen-binding proteins in rat liver. The male rat apparently has two receptors for estrogens, one of which is found in female rats, whereas the other receptor is unique to males. This unique receptor is lost when the animal is castrated and returns under increased testosterone levels. They propose that the extra receptor serves as an estrogen "sponge" and thus protects the male from excess estrogens. Since chronic alcoholics have low levels of testosterone and would theoretically have low levels of estrogen receptors, the clearance of estrogens from the body would be lowered and cause them to accumulate.

SEX-HORMONE-BINDING GLOBULIN

Van Thiel et al., 1974,[23] found elevated plasma concentrations of sex-hormone-binding globulin (SHBG) in chronic alcoholic men. SHBG has a higher affinity for testosterone than estradiol so increased SHBG decreased free (unbound) testosterone which is the biologically active form of the hormone. It would appear that high SHBG levels may be yet another factor contributing to low plasma testosterone levels in alcoholic males and increased levels of plasma estrogens.

TIME SEQUENCE OF MALE FEMINIZATION

Van Thiel, 1976,[24] proposed a possible time sequence when feminization would occur in alcoholic men (modified by this author due to more recent information since Van Thiel's article). With an increase in alcohol use, testicular testosterone production is reduced and pituitary LH secretion rises. Coincident with this, reversible gonadal injury would occur in normal alcohol consuming men. With continued alcohol abuse, the Leydig cells would be damaged irreversibly, lowering testosterone levels permanently. Next, damage to the hypothalamus results in a lowering of LH levels to within normal ranges in spite of low testosterone levels. In the presence of continued alcohol consumption and hepatic disease, the hepatic clearance of estrogens is reduced and estrogens accumulate. Coincident with the retention of estrogens, sex-hormone-binding globulin concentrations increase in plasma, further lowering the androgen-estrogen ratio, resulting in feminization.

BIOLOGICAL EFFECTS ON FEMALES

In female alcoholics, masculinization is rarely seen and clinical features of hypogonadism are ill-defined.[3] The presentation of fetal alcohol syndrome, as well as recurrent pregnancy difficulties, do occur in female alcoholics. Quantitative literature on gonadal functioning in the female alcoholic is lacking. A number of reports in the 1930s and 1940s noted that chronic alcoholic women complained of menstrual problems such as cycle irregularities, menorrhagia (excess flow) and amenorrhea.[3] In 1981, Katz[25] confirmed that many chronic alcoholic women (31 of 33 questioned) complain of sexual difficulties. Ryback[26] noted that although there were no research efforts going on to study alcohol's effect on endocrine function and sexual behavior in females, it is likely that alcohol-related endocrinologic dysfunction occurs in female alcoholics, since they do share aspects of the same hormone system with men (e.g., estrone, estradiol). He reported that intragastric dosages of ethanol, 8 mg/g/day in female rats, will block the normal estrus cycle in 80 percent of the animals exposed.

Female rats fed a 5 percent ethanol diet for 7 weeks showed a 60 percent reduction in ovarian weight.[27] Ovarian structure was grossly altered, characterized by the absence of corpus hemorrhagicums and corpus albicans. In addition plasma levels of estradiol were significantly reduced (about 30 percent) and progesterone levels were reduced 50 percent. The uterus and oviducts reflected the estrogen deprivation and were significantly reduced.

Hughes et al., 1978,[28] looked at the effects of chronic alcoholism on the hypothalamic-pituitary-gonad function of post-menopausal alcoholic women and found no changes. This may not be the case in pre-menopausal women.

These few reports on alcohol's impact on gonadal function in females, as well as the poor pregnancy outcomes of female alcoholics, support the contention that alcohol causes profound alterations in female sexual function.

HUMAN SEXUAL AROUSAL

Alcohol's influence on sexual function extends far beyond gonadal functioning. The human sexual response has often been thought of more as a "cerebral function" than "gonadal function." For the human, in contrast to the rat, psychogenic sources of stimulation are paramount in the control of human sexual arousal and behavior.[29] The penile strain gauge and vaginal photoplethysmograph (monitors vaginal blood volume and pressure pulse) are considered reliable indicators of human sexual response. Recent research measuring penile tumescence and vaginal pressure pulse found a significant negative linear relationship between alcohol and sexual responsiveness.

ALCOHOL AND SEXUAL AROUSAL IN THE MALE

Small (0.6 ml/kg) or moderate (1.2 ml/kg) amounts of alcohol given to adult male volunteers (age 21-29) resulted in about a ten percent reduction in mean penile tumescence (measured in response to erotic motion-pictures).[30] Peak erection and latency to 20 percent of full erection were not affected. However, after the ingestion of high (1.5 ml/kg) concentrations of alcohol, mean penile tumescence was reduced by 66 percent, mean peak erections were reduced to 40 percent of control levels, and the latency period to 20 percent full erection was increased from 4.5 minutes to 8.5 minutes. The primary effect of lower amounts of alcohol was on the maintenance of tumescence rather than the speed or degree of arousal attained. Bridell and Wilson, 1976,[31] also found that the duration of penile response may be more vulnerable to the inhibiting effects of alcohol than the rate or degree (amplitude) of the erectile response.

Prior to these experiments, about 55 percent of the subjects reported that they believed alcohol would enhance their sexual responding and they maintained this belief at the end of the experiment. The fact that alcohol reduced their arousal under the controlled-laboratory conditions did not necessarily indicate that their verbal reports were unreliable. Rather, the discrepancy emphasizes the difficulty in reconciling objective laboratory data with subjective interpretations.

PSYCHOGENIC EFFECT OF ALCOHOL

The theory that the actual physiological arousal might not be necessary for emotional (psychogenic) arousal, provided the individual believes that he is aroused, was examined by Wilson and Lawson, 1976.[32] They divided their experimental population of 40 undergraduate male volunteers (18-22 years old), all social drinkers, into those who expected alcohol or expected tonic water and received what they expected, versus those who expected alcohol or tonic water but received the opposite beverage. The alcohol content was 0.5 g/kg; within the moderate range to facilitate disguising the real alcohol drinks. Subjects who believed they received an alcoholic beverage showed significantly greater mean penile diameter in response to erotic films than those who believed they consumed a non-alcoholic drink, regardless of actual content of their drinks. These results dispute the notion that alcohol influences behavior through a physiologically based disinhibition mechanism. Rather, it appears that at moderate alcohol levels expectancies may determine sexual arousal.

Wilson and Lawson, 1976,[33] using university women, instructed half of them that alcohol would increase their sexual arousal in response to an erotic film, the other half that alcohol would decrease their sexual arousal. Measures of vaginal pressure pulse showed a significant negative relation with alcohol dose. At alcohol concentrations of 0.05 g/kg, pressures measured 50 percent over baseline whereas concentrations of 0.75 g/kg decreased vaginal pressures to a little over 25 percent of baseline. In contrast to the male studies, the females who were instructed that alcohol increased their sexual responsiveness actually experienced less arousal than the group informed alcohol would decrease their arousal. The researchers attributed these results to performance pressure induced by the demands of the experiment.

In 1978, Wilson and Lawson[34] tested the expectancy factor in females using the same format tested for males. Half the subjects who expected alcohol received it, and half who didn't expect alcohol received it. In contrast to the male study, the two groups that received alcohol regardless of whether they believed their drinks contained alcohol showed significantly reduced sexual arousal when viewing erotic films.

Wilson and Lawson (1978)[34] speculated at length on what may contribute to the greater cognitive control of sexual arousal in men versus women. They argue that people have to learn to be sexual. This sexual learning includes linking cognitive and imagery processes to sexual feeling and behavior. Traditionally, society's double standard in regard to sexuality has been more permissive to males than females. Secondly, they propose that women may be at a biological disadvantage in cognitive control of their sexual feelings. Erection in the male is external and visible whereas vaginal arousal is internal, with few cues to facilitate conscious discrimination. This may make accurate sexual labeling of genital sensations more difficult and retard learned associations between cognitive variables like expectancies and genital responses. These theories sound logical but one only need look at other data[30] to recall that males had also expected an increase in sexual arousal contrary to actual laboratory data.

Malatesta et al., 1982,[35] (testing 18 university women) confirmed Wilson and Lawson's[33,34] findings that even though alcohol depressed physiological sexual functioning, the subjects viewed their sexual experience as more pleasurable after alcoholic consumption.

ALCOHOL AND SEXUAL AROUSAL IN THE FEMALE

In 1979, Beckman[36] surveyed 120 women alcoholics and 120 non-alcoholic women as to the perceived effects of alcohol on their sexual responsiveness. Women alcoholics were more likely than non-alcoholics to report that they desire, engage in, and enjoy sexual intercourse more after drinking. It should be noted that 40 percent of the women alcoholics did not feel alcohol enhanced their sexuality. Zucker et al., 1981[37] reported that women alcoholics may not have greater sex-role conflicts than other women, and may be more sexually promiscuous due to problems in interpersonal relationships rather than because of any increase in sexual arousal.

SPOUSE'S ROLE IN DYSFUNCTION

Another factor which may be equally as powerful in producing sexual difficulties for the alcoholic is the deterioration of the relationship with the sex partner.[38] Spouses of alcoholics often show a decreased interest in lovemaking for a number of reasons. Inattention to personal hygiene on the part of the alcoholic decreases attractiveness. Alcoholics frequently are not sensitive to their spouses' needs and can cause stored-up resentment in the non-alcoholic spouse which can be expressed through lack of sexual interest. The alcoholic spouse also may avoid sexual activity because of impotency in the male alcoholic or low libido and non-orgasmic functioning in the female alcoholic. The non-alcoholic spouse may misinterpret this loss of sexual interest in their alcoholic spouse as loss of love or that the alcoholic spouse is sexually involved with someone else. Depression in the alcoholic and/or his spouse may compound the sexual difficulties.

SUMMARY

In males, alcohol has been shown to alter testosterone and estrogen levels which in conjunction with social and psychosocial difficulties can lead the alcoholic into sexual difficulties. In females, alcohol's effects on hormone levels are less well researched but in all probability are also altered. The social and psychosocial difficulties caused by alcohol are manifested in females as well, but their patterns may not necessarily coincide with that of males due to differences in "sexual socialization."

For the non-alcoholic, the crucial effect of small amounts of alcohol may not be on specific physiological responses but on a set of social role conditions which legitimize actions that otherwise would not occur. In this sense alcohol acts as a cue for sexual behavior. To a large extent, it is not in the biochemistry of small quantities of alcohol, but in the person's social learning behavior which under certain circumstances links alcohol and human sexual behavior.

REFERENCES

1. Hammond DC, Milgram GG, Franek B. Sexual Medicine for Alcoholics. *Sexual Medicine Today* 1981; 5:26-27.

2. Scheiner AP, Donovan CM, Bartoshevsky LE. Fetal Alcohol Syndrome in Children Whose Parents Had Stopped Drinking. *Lancet* 1979; 1:1077.

3. Morgan MY. Sex and Alcohol. *Brit Med Bull* 1982; 38:43-52.

4. U.S. Department of Health and Human Services. *Fourth Special Report to the U.S. Congress on Alcohol and Health.* Deluca JR, ed. DHHS Pub. N. (ADM) 81-1080. Washington, DC: Superintendent of Documents, U.S. Government Printing Office, 1981.

5. Van Thiel DH, Lester R. Sex and Alcohol. *Science* 1974; 291:251-253.

6. Ellingboe J, Varanelli CC. Ethanol Inhibits Testosterone Biosynthesis by Direct Action on Leydig Cells. *Res Comm Chem Path Pharm* 1970; 24:87-102.

7. Cicero TJ, Bell RD, Meyer ER. Direct Effects of Ethanol and Acetaldehyde on Testicular Steroidogenesis. *Fed Proc* 1979; 38:428.

8. Van Thiel DH, Gavaler JS, Lester R, et al. Alcohol-Induced Testicular Atrophy. *Gastroenterology* 1975; 69:326-332.

9. Cicero TJ, Meyer ED, Bell RD. Effects of Ethanol on the Hypothalamic Pituitary Luteinizing Hormone Axis and Testicular Steroidogenesis. *J Pharm Exp Ther* 1979; 208: 210-215.

10. Mendelson JH, Mello NK, Ellingboe J. Effects of Acute Alcohol Intake on Pituitary Gonadal Hormones in Normal Human Males. *J Pharm Exp Ther* 1977; 202:676-682.

11. Gordon GG, Altman K, Southern AL, et al. Effect of Alcohol (Ethanol) Administration on Sex Hormone Metabolism in Normal Men. *N Engl J Med* 1976; 295:793-797.

12. Bach FM, Smith MS, Dalterio SL, et al. Role of the Pituitary and the Adrenals in Mediating the Effects of Alcohol on Testicular Steroidogenesis in Mice. *Steroids* 1979; 34: 477-482.

13. Rubin E, Lieber CS, Altman K, et al. Prolonged Ethanol Consumption Increases Testosterone Metabolism in the Liver. *Science* 1976; 191:563-564.

14. Gordon GG, Vittek J, Southern AL, et al. Effects of Chronic Alcohol Ingestion on the Biosynthesis of Steroids in Rat Testicular Homogenate In Vitro. *Endocrinology* 1980; 106:1880-1885.

15. Van Thiel DH, Sherins RJ, Lester R. Mechanism of Hypogonadism in Alcoholic Liver Disease. *Gastroenterology* 1973; 65:574.

16. Bach FM, Bartke A. Effect of Ethyl Alcohol on Plasma Testosterone Level in Mice. *Steroids* 1974; 23:921-927.

17. Mendelson JH, Ellingboe J, Mallo NK. Ethanol Induced Alterations in Pituitary Gonadal Hormones in Human Males. In: Begleiter H. Ed. *Adv in Exp Med and Biology.* New York: Plenum Press, 1980:485-497.

18. Badr FM, Bartke A, Dalterio S, et al. Suppression of Testosterone Production by Ethyl Alcohol. Possible Mode of Action. *Steroids* 1977; 30:647-655.

19. Hafez ES. *Human Reproduction,* 2nd ed. New York: Harper and Row Publishers, 1980.

20. Mezey E, Holt PR. The Inhibition Effect of Ethanol on Retinol Oxidation by Human Liver and Cattle Retina. *Ex Med Pathol* 1971; 15:148-156.

21. Lundholm J, Fabricius-Bjerre N, Bhensen M. Sex Steroids and Sex Hormone Binding Globulin in Males with Chronic Alcoholism. *Eur J Clin Invest* 1978; 8:273-276.

22. Eagon PK, Fischer SE, Imhoff AF, et al. Estrogen Binding Proteins of Male Rat Liver: Influenced by Hormonal Changes. *Arch Biochem Biophys* 1980; 201:486-499.

23. Van Thiel DH, Lester R, Sherins RJ. Hypogonadism in Alcoholic Liver Disease: Evidence for a Double Defect. *Gastroenterology* 1974; 67:1188-1199.

24. Van Thiel DH. Testicular Atrophy and Other Changes in Alcoholic Men. *Med Asp Hum Sex* 1976; 10:153-154.

25. Katz A, Morgan MY, Sherlock S. Alcoholism Treatment in a Medical Setting. *J Stud Alcohol* 1981; 42:136-143.

26. Ryback RS. Chronic Alcohol Consumption and Menstruation. *JAMA* 1977; 238: 2143.

27. Van Thiel DH, Gavaler JS, Lester R. Alcohol Induced Ovarian Failure in the Rat. *J Clin Invest* 1978; 61:624-632.

28. Hughes JN, Perret G, Adessi G, et al. Effects of Chronic Alcoholism on the Pituitary Gonadal Function of Women During Menopausal Transition and in the Post Menopausal Period. *Biomedicine* 1978; 29:279-283.

29. Wilson T. Alcohol and Human Sexual Behavior. *Behav Res and Ther* 1977; 15: 239-252.

30. Rubin HB, Hensen DE. Effects of Alcohol on Male Sexual Responding. *Psychopharmacology* 1976; 47:123-134.

31. Briddell DW, Wilson GT. Effects of Alcohol and Expectancy Set on Male Sexual Arousal. *J Abnormal Psych* 1976; 85:225-234.

32. Wilson GT, Lawson DM. Expectancies, Alcohol, and Sexual Arousal in Male Social Drinkers. *J Abnormal Psych* 1976; 85:587-594.

33. Wilson GT, Lawson DM. Effects of Alcohol on Sexual Arousal in Women. *J Abnormal Psych* 1976; 85:489-497.

34. Wilson GT, Lawson DM. Expectancies, Alcohol, and Sexual Arousal in Women. *J Abnormal Psych* 1978; 87:358-367.

35. Malatesta VJ, Pollack RH, Crotty TD. Acute Alcohol Intoxication and Female Orgasmic Response. *J Sex Res* 1982; 18:1-17.

36. Beckman LJ. Reported Effects of Alcohol on the Sexual Feelings and Behavior of Women Alcoholics and Nonalcoholics. *J Stud Alcohol* 1979; 40:272-282.

37. Zucker RA, Battistich VA, Langer GB. Sexual Behavior, Sex Role Adaptation and Drinking in Young Women. *J Stud Alcohol* 1981; 42:457-465.

38. Parades A. Marital Sexual Factors in Alcoholism. *Med Asp Hum Sex* 1973; 7: 98-115.

Preferred Resources for Help with a Drug Problem among Youths Living in Different Inner City Neighborhood Settings

Richard Dembo, PhD
James Schmeidler, PhD
Robert W. Taylor, PhD
David Agresti, EdD
William Burgos, DSW

ABSTRACT. This paper focuses on the perceived value of various resources to assist youths with a drug problem. An analysis of data gathered in a survey of minority youths attending an inner city, junior high school found that resource preference varied according to their degree of drug involvement and the type of neighborhood

Richard Dembo is with the Department of Criminal Justice, University of South Florida, Tampa, Florida 33620. James Schmeidler is with the New York Division of Substance Abuse Services, Office of Alcoholism and Substance Abuse, Two World Trade Center, New York, NY 10047. Robert W. Taylor and David Agresti are with the Department of Criminal Justice, University of South Florida, Tampa, Florida 33620. William Burgos is with the Department of Psychology, Inter-American University, Hato Rey, Puerto Rico 00919. Address reprint requests to Richard Dembo.

This research was supported in part by a grant from the University of South Florida Research and Creative Scholarship Fund.

We are grateful for the assistance given us by the principal, teachers and parents of the junior high school who must remain anonymous. The reactions of many youngsters to earlier versions of the survey instruments were valuable to our research effort. The support and encouragement of the New York State Office of Drug Abuse Services, and especially Douglas S. Lipton, Director of the Division of Cost Effectiveness and Research, are appreciated. Ken Marion, Dean Babst, Sharon Diamond, Carol Spielman and Phyllis Bergman were helpful in processing the data. However, these persons are not responsible for the views that are expressed in the paper or the ways in which the data were examined.

We also appreciate the help of the University of South Florida's word processing unit in the preparation of this manuscript. Ms. Magdalene Deutsch was very helpful in typing the tables.

We would like to thank Dr. Louise G. Richards, Division of Research, National Institute on Drug Abuse, for initially suggesting we pursue the line of analysis of which this paper is one product.

© 1983 by The Haworth Press, Inc. All rights reserved.

setting in which they perceived they lived. The youths expressed broad support for traditional, institutional representatives in dealing with drug problems. However, as the level of perceived toughness/drug use in their neighborhoods, and their degree of drug involvement, increased, the youths tended to rely more on peers as drug problem aides. Implications of these findings for future drug abuse prevention and intervention strategies among youths in the inner city are drawn.

INTRODUCTION

As the drug field has become theoretically and methodologically more sophisticated, there has been an increasing recognition of the importance of contextual effects on the correlates and processes of individuals' drug use.[1-5] In shifting attention away from the drug user, who is seen as carrying a personal set of demographic, psychological, and socio-cultural characteristics constraining him/her to drug use, focus has come to rest on the interactions occurring among these sets of variables and environmental setting in regard to their relative impact, and networks of causal influences, on drug use. Appreciation of the importance of environmental context in understanding such psychosocial behavior as drug use promises to increase our insight into the etiology of this behavior in various social settings. In addition, this research focus can be expected to lead to the establishment of effective drug abuse prevention strategies in two key ways.

First, this thrust will lead to the establishment of a theoretical grounding that can inform the creation of effective and engaging drug abuse prevention programs for various high risk groups. Such a development would deal creatively with a recognized deficiency in drug abuse prevention programming, which has generally failed to incorporate knowledge of the psychological, social and cultural features of the lives of various groups into prevention programs that are addressed to them.[6,7] Second, this line of work can lead to the efficient identification of individuals and groups at high risk of becoming seriously involved in drug taking, and experiencing adverse personal and social consequences of this behavior.[8]

There is a special need to understand more fully the drug use experiences of adolescents living in inner city areas, and to develop effective and engaging drug abuse prevention for them. It is in these settings that the risks of drug use and adverse effects of drug taking are perceived to be greatest.[9-11]

The present paper is a modest step in this direction. Developing from previous analyses, which highlight that different correlates and processes are involved in the drug use of a sample of inner city youths who characterize their neighborhood settings as having different degrees of toughness/drug use,[12-14] the paper examines various resources drug involved youths living in these settings would use for help with a drug problem. In this effort, we heuristically test the following hypothesis:

> Drug involved youths living in low, medium and high toughness/drug use neighborhoods would approach different resources for help with a drug problem.

Our findings highlight that important differences exist in the resources that would be used by youths with differing degrees of drug involvement in the three settings. Results also indicate that youths at different levels of drug use would approach different resources for help with a drug problem in the various settings. Additional analyses suggest ways in which effective and engaging drug abuse prevention activities can be developed for youths living in high toughness/drug neighborhoods. Implications of these findings for future research and drug abuse prevention and intervention work among inner city youths are elaborated.

METHOD

The data we report were gathered in the second wave of a two-part survey of youths attending an inner city junior high school in the South Bronx, New York City. Completed in the winter 1976, the survey was invited by school officials and local school board members. It was believed that information obtained on the amount, patterns and correlates of the students' drug use would lead to the development of effective and engaging drug abuse prevention programs in the school.

Extensive exploratory work among youths living in neighborhoods similar to those covered by the school preceded the development of the questionnaires that were used. In addition, panels of youths attending schools other than the one where we planned to conduct the survey completed and critiqued draft versions of the instruments.

Student interest in the confidential, voluntary survey is reflected in the high rate of participation. Administered in the youths' social studies classrooms in one period, over 97% of the students in class at the time of the survey took part. These youths represented 78% (1045) of the 1,344 students enrolled in the school.

Since the sample was not a probability sample of youths in the community or school, inferences concerning the community cannot be drawn from our data. However, tests of significance were performed as a heuristic device to highlight relationships.

DESCRIPTION OF THE SAMPLE

Table 1 sets out the demographic characteristics of the youths participating in the survey. Somewhat more girls than boys participated in the survey. The youths averaged 13 years of age. While residence in mother headed households was relatively frequent, most of the youngsters resided with both their parents. The vast majority of the youths were either Puerto Rican or Black. Although socioeconomic status (SES) information was not available for 41% of the youths, the data we do have indicate the families represented by the youths in the survey tend to be of low to moderate SES.

DRUG USE

The survey probed the youths' use of the following seven categories of drugs: (1) alcohol, (2) marijuana (including hashish), (3) LSD or similar substances, (4) depressants, (5) narcotics, (6) solvents and (7) stimulants. (Although questions were asked about the

Table 1

Demographic Description of the Sample (N=1045)

Sex: male = 46%, female = 52%, no response = 2%.

Age ($\bar{x}$): 13 years (SD = 1.11)

Home Composition: living with both parents = 56%; living with mother = 36%; living with father = 1%; living with neither parent = 3%; no response = 4%.

Ethnicity: Puerto Rican = 43%; Black = 41%; Other Hispanic (e.g., Cuban, Columbian) =3%; White = 6%; "Other" (mainly Oriental) = 3%; no response = 3%.

Socioeconomic Status — SES (measured by educational level of household head): 8th grade or less = 8%; some high school = 11%; high school graduate = 20%; some college = 7%; college graduate = 9%; attended graduate or professional school = 4%; don't know/no answer = 41%.

---

use of tobacco, these data are not reported here.) With the exception of alcohol and marijuana, less than 7% of the youths claimed they had used any of the drugs in the last five categories. On the other hand, 46% and 24% of the youths, respectively, claimed they had used alcohol and marijuana one or more time during their lives; and 33% noted they had used alcohol, and 19% marijuana, during the six month period prior to the survey.

Our analysis of the drug use data focussed on the development of a measure of drug involvement. This interest, coupled with a concern to uncover the current drug use experiences of the youths, led us to pursue a Guttman analysis of their claimed drug use during the six month period prior to the survey. Results indicated the data forming the four category scale were strongly unidimensional, having high reproducibility (.954) and scalability (.806) coefficients (the minimum marginal reproducibility for the scale is .764).

Failure to complete a sufficient number of items or inconsistent responses to different questions about the same drugs eliminated 20% of the 1,045 youths from placement in one of the Guttman scale categories. The remaining 831 youths were located into one of the following four categories on the basis of the most "extreme" drug used:

1. all use denied (N = 437, 53%);
2. use of alcohol admitted (N = 194, 23%);
3. use of marijuana—and usually alcohol—admitted (N = 146, 18%);
4. claimed use of other substances—and usually alcohol and marijuana (N = 54, 6%).

This drug involvement scale is similar to the index developed by Single, Kandel and Faust.[15,16] The drug use data should be regarded as a conservative estimate of this behavior among the students. Twenty-two percent of the youths enrolled in the school are not represented in the survey data. Previous research has shown that youths who do not attend school regularly tend to use drugs more often than those who do.[17]

RESOURCES FOR HELP WITH A DRUG PROBLEM

Previous research has indicated that youths who are more involved with drugs tend to rely less on family, professional and various institutional (e.g., teacher, police officer) resources for help with a drug problem, and more on drug using peers and former users.[18] Drawing upon this work, respondents were asked to indicate if they "would go," "would not go," or were "not sure or didn't know" whether they would go to each of the resources listed in Table 2 for help with a drug problem. Factor analysis of the youths' replies to the twelve items found limited common variance among them, resulting in our decision to examine each resource individually.

PERCEPTIONS OF THE NEIGHBORHOOD

Based on previous research, thirteen items were created to probe the youths' views of various aspects of their neighborhoods.[19] Principal factor analysis of the youths' replies to the items was first pursued; this was followed by a varimax rotation of the three factors emerging from the principal factor analysis. One factor relevant to our interest emerged from this analysis.

Labelled *toughness/drug use,* items probing how "tough" it is to get along in one's neighborhood, that people tend to get into fights, that it's hard avoiding "trouble" growing up in the neighborhood, that the neighborhood contains a lot of gangs, and that young people are into popping pills and getting high on pot have high, positive loadings on this factor. An item probing how "peaceful" it is to live in the neighborhood has a strong, negative loading on the factor.

In order to use as much data as possible in the analyses, factor scores were developed for this cluster using a zero (the Z-score mean) for a nonresponse. Mean value substitution was not performed for youths not answering any of the items. (Analysis found no significant demographic or drug use differences to exist between youths not answering any of the questions and those responding to one or more items.) In order to identify neighborhood settings of different degrees of perceived toughness/drug use, the factor scores were objectively divided into three, equal sized groups (low, medium and high toughness/drug use).

We appreciate that individuals' perceptions of their environment are partly determined by the attitudes and values these perceptions are assumed to determine.[20] However, studies indicate the use of these data is less bias producing than might be supposed.[21,22] Further, Clayton and Voss' recent study leads them to assert that an individual's "subjective perception of the environment may be as important in explaining his behavior as the objective characteristics of that environment."[23]

RESULTS

Correlates of Resources to be Sought for Help with a Drug Problem

Prior to conducting the major analyses reported in this paper, examination was made of the possible relationship between the youths' ethnicity, their degree of drug involvement, resources they would approach for help with a drug problem and their perceptions of the toughness/drug use in their neighborhoods.[24] No substantial effects were found. Accordingly, subsequent analyses included youths from all five ethnic groups.

Table 2 gives the percent of students overall, and those living in the three toughness/drug use settings, who would go to each of the twelve resources for help with a drug problem. The overall results indicate that only a member of one's family, staff member of a drug program and a doctor would be approached for assistance with a drug problem by a majority of the youths.

Table 2 also shows a statistically significant decline in the percentage of youths indicating they would seek a staff member of a drug program, and the school drug education teacher, for help with a drug problem as we move from the low to the high toughness/drug use setting. A similar, marginally significant, decline appears in regard to a willingness to go to a doctor for assistance with a drug problem.

Previous analyses of this data set indicated that youths living in high toughness/drug use settings are at greater risk of initiating drug use, and experiencing adverse personal and social consequences of their drug taking. Hence, a further analysis was pursued, comparing youths' living in high, with those living in low or medium, toughness/drug use neighborhoods. The across-the-three-neighborhood-setting trends were replicated in these analyses. In addition, there was a marginally significant tendency for youths living in high toughness/drug use areas, when compared to those residing in low or medium toughness/drug use settings, to claim a willingness to approach a former drug user for help with a drug problem ($X^2 = 3.40$, df = 1,

Table 2

Resources That Would Be Sought for Help with a Drug Problem
in the Three Toughness/Drug Use Neighborhood Settings - in Percent
Overall Results

Resource	Total	Neighborhood Setting			Chi-Square*
		Low Toughness/Drug Use	Medium Toughness/Drug Use	High Toughness/Drug Use	
A member of my family	53% (n=906)	55% (n=309)	53% (n=295)	51% (n=302)	N.S.
Police Officer	24% (n=893)	28% (n=307)	21% (n=288)	23% (n=298)	N.S.
Staff member of a drug program	63% (n=901)	67% (n=308)	65% (n=292)	56% (n=301)	$x^2 = 8.36$ df = 2, p < .02
Doctor	69% (n=887)	73% (n=305)	70% (n=287)	64% (n=295)	$x^2 = 5.47$ df = 2, .10>p>.05
The drug education teacher in this school	49% (n=894)	56% (n=305)	47% (n=289)	43% (n=300)	$x^2 = 10.82$ df = 2, p < .01
Some other teacher in this school	19% (n=888)	20% (n=305)	19% (n=288)	19% (n=295)	N.S.
A friend who does not use drugs	37% (n=894)	36% (n=304)	38% (n=291)	38% (n=299)	N.S.
A former drug user	31% (n=897)	28% (n=306)	29% (n=290)	35% (n=301)	N.S.
Neighbor	17% (n=894)	19% (n=305)	16% (n=290)	16% (n=299)	N.S.
A friend who uses drugs	11% (n=888)	11% (n=303)	10% (n=289)	14% (n=296)	N.S.
Priest, minister, or rabbi	30% (n=889)	32% (n=303)	29% (n=289)	28% (n=297)	N.S.
Social worker	21% (n=894)	25% (n=305)	19% (n=290)	19% (n=299)	N.S.

*These tests involve a dichotomous representation of the resource variables (i.e., would go to for help vs would not go to or don't know/ not sure).

.10 > p > .05). (Detailed information on these analyses is available from the senior author upon request.)

In terms of the hypothesis informing our analyses, more interesting findings emerge when we compare the relationships between the youths' drug involvement and the resources they would approach for help with a drug problem across the three neighborhood settings. Two major conclusions can be drawn from the results shown in Tables 3A, 3B, and 3C.

First, the number of significant relationships between the youths' drug involvement and their willingness to approach various resources for help with a drug problem increase as we go from the low and medium to high toughness/drug use settings. This clearer delineation of "appropriate" and "inappropriate" drug abuse resource preferences among youths living in high toughness/drug use neighborhoods may be seen as one reflection of the more deep rooted nature of the drug use subcultures existing in these areas.

Second, in support of our hypothesis, there are important differences in the correlations between the youths' drug involvement and their claimed willingness to use the various resources for help with a drug problem across the three neighborhood settings. Among youths living in low toughness/drug use neighborhoods, those who are more involved with drugs are significantly less likely to approach a police officer, doctor or non-drug using friend for help with a drug problem, than their less drug involved peers.

Negative relationships are found between drug involvement and willingness to go to a family member or a police officer for assistance with a drug problem among youths living in medium toughness/drug use neighborhoods. On the other hand, youngsters who are drug involved are more willing to seek out a former drug user for help with a drug problem, than are their less drug involved peers.

In high toughness/drug use settings, negative relationships are found between youths' drug involvement and their preference for a family member, police officer, staff member of a drug program, doctor, school drug education teacher, non-drug using friend, and a priest, minister or rabbi to help with a drug problem. On the other hand, drug involved youths are significantly more likely to approach a drug using friend for help with a drug problem, than youngsters who are not into drug taking.

The disinclination of drug involved youths living in high toughness/drug use neighborhoods to seek out a drug program staff member, doctor or school drug education teacher for assistance with a

Table 3A, 3B, and 3C

Correlations(r) Among the Youths' Demographic, Drug Use, and Felt Credibility Characteristics and Their Willingness to Use Various Resources for Help with a Drug Problem in Low, Medium, and High Toughness/Drug Use Neighborhoods[a]

Table 3A: Low Toughness/Drug Use Setting

	Family Member	Police Officer	Drug Program Staff Member	Doctor	School Drug Education Teacher	Other Teacher in School	Non-Drug Using Friend	Former Drug User	Neighbor	Drug Using Friend	Priest, Minister or Rabbi	Social Worker
Age	-.057 (n=309)	-.083 (n=307)	.005 (n=308)	-.084 (n=305)	-.023 (n=305)	.015 (n=305)	-.042 (n=304)	-.039 (n=306)	-.103 (n=305)	-.024 (n=303)	.049 (n=303)	.063 (n=305)
Sex	-.020 (n=307)	-.118* (n=305)	.012 (n=306)	-.004 (n=303)	.024 (n=303)	-.010 (n=303)	.054 (n=302)	-.035 (n=304)	-.074 (n=303)	.039 (n=301)	-.019 (n=303)	-.028 (n=303)
Home Composition	-.103 (n=297)	-.119* (n=296)	-.059 (n=296)	-.048 (n=294)	-.101 (n=293)	-.020 (n=294)	.033 (n=293)	.078 (n=295)	.006 (n=294)	.141 (n=293)	-.021 (n=292)	-.013 (n=294)
Education Level of Household Head	.037 (n=206)	-.070 (n=207)	-.048 (n=206)	.108 (n=206)	-.066 (n=204)	-.058 (n=205)	-.040 (n=204)	-.024 (n=207)	-.030 (n=207)	.008 (n=205)	.017 (n=204)	.034 (n=205)
Drug Involvement	-.092 (n=275)	-.131* (n=274)	-.002 (n=275)	-.134[*] (n=272)	-.118 (n=271)	-.083 (n=271)	-.162** (n=271)	.033 (n=272)	-.037 (n=272)	.072 (n=271)	-.062 (n=269)	-.106 (n=272)
Reliability of Resource as Source of Information on Drugs	.164** (n=300)	.262*** (n=301)	.309*** (n=303)	.246*** (n=299)	.346*** (n=299)	.348*** (n=298)	.232*** (n=300)	.368*** (n=301)	.283*** (n=296)	.193*** (n=294)	.539*** (n=297)	.515*** (n=298)

Table 3B

Table 3B: Medium Toughness/Drug Use Setting

	Family Member	Police Officer	Drug Program Staff Member	Doctor	School Drug Education Teacher	Other Teacher in School	Non-Drug Using Friend	Former Drug User	Neighbor	Drug Using Friend	Priest, Minister or Rabbi	Social Worker
Age	-.062 (n=296)	-.081 (n=290)	-.016 (n=294)	-.096 (n=289)	-.020 (n=291)	-.013 (n=290)	-.098 (n=293)	-.078 (n=292)	-.052 (n=292)	.066 (n=291)	-.112 (n=291)	.039 (n=292)
Sex	-.039 (n=292)	-.214*** (n=286)	-.028 (n=290)	-.060 (n=285)	-.010 (n=287)	-.073 (n=286)	.086 (n=289)	-.089 (n=288)	-.113 (n=288)	.042 (n=288)	-.090 (n=287)	.067 (n=288)
Home Composition	-.089 (n=292)	-.056 (n=286)	-.031 (n=290)	-.041 (n=285)	.111 (n=287)	-.050 (n=286)	.004 (n=289)	-.007 (n=288)	-.009 (n=288)	-.014 (n=287)	-.003 (n=287)	-.026 (n=288)
Education Level of Household Head	.009 (n=176)	.045 (n=173)	.098 (n=176)	.001 (n=172)	.057 (n=175)	.076 (n=172)	-.096 (n=176)	-.008 (n=176)	.124 (n=175)	.058 (n=175)	.011 (n=175)	.155* (n=176)
Drug Involvement	-.155[*] (n=255)	-.204*** (n=251)	.072 (n=254)	-.073 (n=249)	-.080 (n=252)	-.052 (n=250)	-.022 (n=254)	.200*** (n=253)	-.053 (n=252)	.020 (n=253)	-.055 (n=251)	.099 (n=252)
Reliability of Resource As Source of Information on Drugs	.195*** (n=291)	.256*** (n=286)	.261*** (n=286)	.290*** (n=285)	.361*** (n=284)	.384*** (n=284)	.112 (n=289)	.310*** (n=288)	.277*** (n=287)	.201*** (n=287)	.345*** (n=279)	.418*** (n=283)

67

Table 3C:

Table 3C: High Toughness/Drug Use Setting

	Family Member	Police Officer	Drug Program Staff Member	Doctor	School Drug Education Teacher	Other Teacher in School	Non-Drug Using Friend	Former Drug User	Neighbor	Drug Using Friend	Priest, Minister or Rabbi	Social Worker
Age	-.139* (n=301)	-.080 (n=297)	-.111 (n=300)	-.055 (n=294)	-.056 (n=299)	.052 (n=294)	-.091 (n=298)	.031 (n=300)	-.007 (n=298)	.092 (n=295)	.025 (n=296)	-.034 (n=298)
Sex	.003 (n=294)	-.126* (n=290)	.142* (n=293)	.106 (n=287)	.107 (n=292)	-.032 (n=287)	.071 (n=291)	.059 (n=293)	.048 (n=291)	-.020 (n=288)	.022 (n=290)	.109 (n=292)
Home Composition	-.074 (n=293)	-.061 (n=289)	-.033 (n=292)	.014 (n=287)	.001 (n=291)	-.085 (n=286)	.006 (n=290)	-.175*** (n=292)	-.080 (n=291)	-.053 (n=288)	-.084 (n=289)	.051 (n=291)
Education Level of Household Head	.005 (n=167)	-.067 (n=168)	.049 (n=168)	.016 (n=165)	-.043 (n=167)	-.154* (n=167)	.122 (n=168)	.052 (n=167)	.000 (n=169)	.042 (n=167)	-.133 (n=167)	-.024 (n=168)
Drug Involvement	-.201[***] (n=253)	-.221*** (n=250)	-.163[**] (n=253)	-.261*** (n=248)	-.211*** (n=251)	-.002 (n=247)	-.131[*] (n=253)	.012 (n=253)	-.002 (n=254)	.127* (n=248)	-.124[*] (n=251)	-.028 (n=253)
Reliability of Resource As Source of Information on Drugs	.135* (n=291)	.271*** (n=290)	.334*** (n=295)	.314*** (n=291)	.304*** (n=286)	.323*** (n=286)	.049 (n=294)	.238*** (n=292)	.333*** (n=291)	.302*** (n=290)	.420*** (n=290)	.491*** (n=291)

a. Non-responses have been excluded from these correlations. The variables used in this analysis were coded as follows:
1. age: 11 years or under = 1, 12 years = 2, 13 years = 3, 14 years = 4, 15 years = 5, 16 years or over =6;
2. sex: male = 1, female = 2;
3. home composition: living with both parents = 1, living with mother or father = 2, living with neither parent = 3;
4. educational level of household head: eighth grade or less = 1, some high school = 2, high school graduate = 3, some college = 4, college graduate = 5, graduate or professional school = 6;
5. drug involvement in last 6 months: all use denied = 1, alcohol use = 2, marijuana use = 3, use of drugs other than alcohol or marijuana = 4;
6. belief in various sources of information on drugs: mostly not believable = 1, don't know = 2, mostly believable = 3;
7. resources to be used for help with a drug problem: would not go to for help = 1, don't know/not sure = 2, would go to for help = 3.

Two-tailed test significance levels:

   * p < .05
  ** p < .01
 *** p < .001

drug problem deserves some comment. While we lack data regarding the reasons for the drug involved youths' rejection of these resources, relevant research suggests drug users in high drug use areas often view these resources with distrust, suspicion and, sometimes, as extensions of the criminal justice system.[25]

There were mutual relationships among the youths' demographic and drug use characteristics and the various resources that would be sought for help with a drug problem. Accordingly, for each neighborhood setting, partial correlations were obtained between the youths' drug involvement and the above noted helping agents, controlling for the youths' demographic characteristics. When this was accomplished, the above reported drug involvement-resources for help with a drug problem relationships remained statistically significant, with the exception of those reported in Tables 3A, 3B and 3C which have bracketed asterisks.

The need for the three separate, perceived neighborhood setting analyses reported in Tables 3A, 3B and 3C is highlighted in a related analysis we performed. Examination of the correlations between the youths' drug involvement and their willingness to approach the various resources for the three settings considered together (or pooled) found smaller magnitudes of association than are reported in Tables 3A, 3B, and 3C. (These results are available from the senior author.)

Believability of Resources and its Use to Help with a Drug Problem

Previous research leads to the expectation that sources of information on drugs that are felt to be credible would be more likely to be approached for assistance with a drug problem, than sources which are felt to provide inaccurate or misleading information on drugs.[26-28] This expectation was examined by studying the relationships between the youths' ratings of the believability of each of the twelve resources as sources of information on drugs, and their willingness to use each for help with a drug problem. As Tables 3A, 3B and 3C show, this expectation was confirmed in each toughness/drug use setting.

Comparison of the believability-resource use correlations with the relationships between the youths' drug involvement and their willingness to use each resource for help with a drug problem highlights an important issue: *with two exceptions, these two sets of relationships operate at cross purposes.* For example, among youths living in low toughness/drug use neighborhoods, drug involvement is negatively associated with their willingness to approach a non-drug using friend for assistance with a drug problem; on the other hand, the credibility of a non-drug using friend as a source of information on drugs is positively related to the youths' preference of this individual to help with a drug problem. Since, with few exceptions, there are low magnitudes of association between the youths' drug involvement and their perceived credibility of the various resources as sources of information on drugs in the three settings, the drug use and believability variables have separate effects on the youths' willingness to use the resources for help with a drug problem.

The analyses reported in Tables 3A, 3B and 3C address the question: For each setting, how does the youths' overall involvement with drugs relate to their potential use of each resource for help with a drug problem? Another, equally important, question asks: What kind(s) of resource(s) would a particular kind of drug using youth approach for help with a drug problem in the three settings? Answers to this question could highlight drug abuse prevention and intervention resources most likely to be accepted by youths at different levels of drug use in the three toughness/drug use neighborhoods. These were the interests underlying an additional analysis of the data we performed.

Level of Drug Use and Willingness to Approach Various Resources for Help with a Drug Problem in the Three Toughness/Drug Use Neighborhood Areas

In order to examine this issue, the analyses reported in Table 2 were repeated for youths' claiming no drug use, alcohol use or the use of marijuana and other drugs (since there are a relatively small number of cases in the latter category, these youths were combined with the marijuana users) during the six months prior to the survey. A summary of the results of these analyses follows. (Due to space concerns, tables reporting these findings have been omitted. Copies of these tables are available from the senior author upon request.)

Non-Drug Users and Alcohol Users

Generally speaking, non-drug users and the users of alcohol reflect similar degrees of willingness to seek out the various resources for help with a drug problem, regardless of the neighborhood setting in which they live. Overall, a staff member of a drug program, doctor and the school drug education teacher would be sought for help with a drug problem by a majority of the non-drug users and the users of alcohol. In addition, a majority of non-drug using youths indicated a willingness to approach a member of their family for such assistance.

Further analyses showed that non-drug using youths living in low toughness/drug use neighborhoods are significantly more likely to approach a drug education teacher ($X^2 = 7.24$, df = 2, p <.03), and alcohol users residing in high toughness/drug use settings significantly more prone to seek out a non-drug using friend ($X^2 = 4.19$, df = 1, p <.05), for help with a drug problem, than their counterparts who live in other neighborhood areas. Importantly, there are no significant differences in the inclination of each of these two groups to approach a drug using friend for assistance with a drug problem across the three settings.

Marijuana and Other Drug Users

Overall, a staff member of a drug program and a doctor would be sought by a majority of these youths for help with a drug problem. Compared to youths living in medium or low toughness/drug use neighborhoods, youngsters in high toughness/drug use settings are significantly less likely to go to a staff member of a drug program for help with a drug problem ($X^2 = 6.26$, df = 1, p <.02); and have a marginally significant disinclination to approach a doctor for this assistance ($X^2 = 3.50$, df = 1, .10 >p >.05). On the other hand, youths in high toughness/drug use areas are significantly more likely to seek out a drug using friend for help with a drug problem ($X^2 = 4.35$, df = 1, p <.05), than youngsters residing in low or medium toughness/drug use neighborhoods. These findings lend further support to our hypothesis, and highlight the influence of the drug use subcultures existing in the high toughness/drug use neighborhoods on the youths' willingness to approach the various resources.

DISCUSSION

The results of our analyses lend support to our hypothesis. While the correlations between the youths' drug involvement and their preferred resources to be sought for help with a drug problem (see

Tables 3A, 3B and 3C) are low to modest in magnitude in the low, medium and high toughness/drug use settings, fourteen of the thirty-six relationships are statistically significant; and eight relationships retain their statistically significant level of association when the youths' background characteristics are controlled.

The construct validity of the results reported in Tables 3A, 3B and 3C is suggested in a number of trends. First, as we go from the low to the high toughness/drug use setting, the greater influence of a drug use subculture (highlighted in previous analyses of this data set[14]) is associated with a clearer delineation between "acceptable" and "unacceptable" resources to be approached for help with a drug problem. Second, the nature of the correlations between the youths' drug involvement and their willingness to seek out the various resources for help with a drug problem in the three neighborhood settings indicates an increased tendency for drug involved youths to avoid family members and various professional-institutional representatives for help with a drug problem, and, instead, to look to drug using peers for this assistance. Third, consistent with the relevant research reviewed earlier, while the felt believability of the various resources as a source of information on drugs is related positively to the youths' willingness to use these resources for assistance with a drug problem, the credibility and drug involvement factors often work at cross-purposes in each of the three settings. Fourth, our level of drug use analyses show an increasing inclination for users of marijuana and other drugs, particularly those living in high toughness/drug use settings, to avoid conventional resources for assistance with a drug problem, favoring, instead, drug using friends for this help.

Clearly, the development of engaging and effective programs to prevent inner city youths from initiating "serious" drug use, or attempting to reverse a deepening involvement in drug taking among youths who are using drugs, requires ethnographically informed strategies which utilize key features of their life-styles. In previous work, we have tried to set out a model for this work.[29-31]

The youths we studied who are not involved in drug use, or are alcohol users, would appear to be good candidates for drug abuse prevention efforts. Our results indicate that these youths would respond rather well to programs that involve such traditional prevention agents as a staff member of a drug program, a doctor or a school based drug education teacher.

The situation is rather different for the users of marijuana and other drugs, particularly those living in high toughness/drug use neighborhoods, where our results suggest the influence of the drug use subculture is greatest. As Kaufman suggests, the process of increased involvement with drugs for these youths can be most effectively reversed by using respected neighborhood residents as role models.[32] In particular, neighborhood residents who have overcome their personal abuse of drugs can, with appropriate training, serve as valuable members of these programs. Such persons can assist in the counseling, and take part in the vocational training, remedial education and job development work, that is needed in these inner city areas. Programs that address the youths' drug use on a clinical and individual level are inappropriate in these settings.

Increased interest in harnessing indigenous community resources in the creation and implementation of drug abuse prevention programs is consistent with the growing appreciation in the drug field that prevention efforts need to work with existing community sociocultural norms in developing social sanctions and rituals reinforcing responsible drug taking; and, where indicated, to develop new norms which devalue the status, and patterns of use, of specific drugs which are at great risk of causing adverse personal and social effects.[33-35]

We need to know much more about how patterns of drug use develop in inner city areas. While this basic research process continues, the need for effective drug abuse prevention and intervention programs in these settings requires an immediate response. The accumulating evidence cited above consistently highlights the importance of drawing upon the features of the lives of the youths who are using drugs in efforts to reduce their risk of dysfunctional drug taking. While difficult, the salutary effects of attempts to develop more ethnographically informed drug abuse prevention and intervention programs constitutes a great intellectual and social policy challenge to drug abuse researchers and program creators. The 1980s promises to be an exciting decade for these developments.

REFERENCES

1. Braucht GN. Psychosocial research on teenage drinking. In: Scarpitti F, Datesman, S, eds. Drugs and the youth culture. Beverly Hills, CA: Sage Press, 1980.

2. Clayton RR, Voss HL. Young men and drugs in manhattan: a causal analysis. Rockville, MD: National Institute on Drug Abuse, 1981.

3. Gersick KE, Grady K, Sexton E, Lyons M. Personality and sociodemographic fac-

tors in adolescent drug use. In: Lettieri D, Lundford J. eds. Drug abuse and the american adolescent. Rockville, MD: National Institute on Drug Abuse, 1981.

4. Kaplan HB. Deviant behavior in defense of self. New York: Academic Press, 1980.

5. Kaufman E. The relationship of social class and ethnicity to drug abuse. In: Smith D, Anderson S. eds.: A multicultural view of drug abuse. Cambridge, MA: Shenkman Press, 1980.

6. Cabinet Committee on Drug Abuse Prevention, Treatment and Rehabilitation. Recommendations for future federal activities in drug abuse prevention. Washington, DC: Govt. Printing Office, 1977.

7. Schaps E, DiBartolo R. Primary prevention evaluation research: a review of 127 program evaluations. Walnut Creek, CA: Pyramid Project—Pacific Institute for Research and Evaluation, 1978.

8. Robins LN, Ratcliff KS. Risk factors in the continuation of childhood antisocial behavior into adulthood. International J. of Mental Health 1978-79;7:96-116.

9. Chambers CD, Inciardi JA. An assessment of drug use in the general population: special report no. 2. Albany, N.Y.: N.Y.S. Narcotic Addiction Control Commission, 1971.

10. Rittenhouse JD. ed. The epidemiology of heroin and other narcotics. Rockville, MD: National Institute on Drug Abuse, 1977.

11. Brunswick AF. Health and drug behavior: a study of urban black adolescents. Addictive Diseases: An International Journal 1977;3:197-214.

12. Dembo R, Schmeidler J, Taylor RW, Burgos W. Supports for, and consequences of, early drug involvement among inner city junior high school youths living in three neighborhood settings. J Drug Education 1982;12:191-210.

13. Dembo R, Schmeidler J, Burgos W, Taylor RW. Environmental setting and early drug involvement among inner city junior high school youths 1982, in review.

14. Dembo R, Schmeidler J, Burgos W. Processes of early drug involvement in three inner city neighborhood settings. Deviant Behavior 1982;3:359-383.

15. Kandel DB. Reaching the hard-to-reach: illicit drug use among high school absentees. Addictive Diseases: An International Journal 1975;1:465-480.

16. Smart R. Recent studies of the validity and reliability of self-reported drug use. Canadian J of Criminology and Corrections 1975;17:326-333.

17. Single E, Kandel DB, Faust R. Patterns of multiple drug use in high school. J Health and Social Behavior 1974;15:344-357.

18. Dembo R, Schmeidler J, Lipton DS, Babst DV. A survey of students' awareness of and attitudes toward drug abuse prevention programs in New York State, Winter 1974/75. International J Addictions 1979;14:311-328.

19. Dembo R. Critical factors in understanding adolescent aggression. Social Psychiatry 1973;8:212-219.

20. Kandel DB, Drug and drinking behavior among youth. Annual Review of Sociology 1980;6:235-285.

21. Kandel DB. Some comments on the relationship of selected criteria variables to adolescent illicit drug use. In: Lettieri DJ. ed. Predicting adolescent drug abuse: a review of issues, methods and correlates. Rockville, MD: National Institute on Drug Abuse, 1975.

22. Kandel DB, Kessler RC, Margulies RZ. Antecendents of adolescent initiation into stages of drug use: a developmental analysis. In: Kandel DB. ed. Longitudinal research on drug use. Washington DC: Hemisphere Press, 1978.

23. Clayton RR, Voss HL. Young men and drugs in manhattan: a causal analysis. Rockville, MD: National Institute on Drug Abuse, 1981:114.

24. Dembo R, Burgos W, Des Jarlais D, Schmeidler J. Ethnicity and drug use among junior high school youths. International J Addictions 1979;14:557-568.

25. For an example, see Feldman HW, Waldorf D. Angel dust in four american cities: an ethnographic study of pcp users. Rockville, MD: National Institute on Drug Abuse, 1980.

26. Fejer D, Smart RG, Whitehead PC, LaForest L. Sources of information about drugs among high school students. Public Opinion Q 1971;35:235-241.

27. Sinnett ER, Press A, Bates RA, Harvey WM. Credibility of sources of information about drugs. Psychological Reports 1975;36:299-309.

28. Dembo R, Schmeidler J, Babst DV, Lipton DS. Drug information source credibility among junior and senior high school youths. American J of Drug and Alcohol Abuse 1977; 4:43-54.

29. Dembo R, Burgos W. A framework for developing drug abuse prevention strategies for young people in ghetto areas. J Drug Education 1976;6:313-325.

30. Dembo R, Burgos W, Babst D, Schmeidler J, LaGrand L. Neighborhood relationships and drug involvement among inner city junior high school youths: implications for drug education and prevention programming. J Drug Education 1978;8:231-252.

31. Dembo R.: Critical issues and experiences in drug treatment and prevention evaluation. International J. Addictions 1982;16:1399-1414.

32. Kaufman E. The relationship of social class and ethnicity to drug abuse. In: Smith DE, Anderson SM. eds. A multicultural view of drug abuse. Cambridge, MA: Shenkham Press, 1978.

33. Zinberg NE, Jacobson RC, Harding WM. Social sanctions and rituals as a basis of drug abuse prevention. American J Drug and Alcohol Abuse 1975;2:165-182.

34. Jacobson RC, Zinberg NE. The social basis of drug abuse prevention. Washington, DC: Drug Abuse Council, 1975.

35. Boyle JM, Brunswick AF. What happened in harlem? an analysis of a decline in heroin use among a generation unit of urban black youth. J Drug Issues 1980;10:109-130.

The Family in the Etiology and Treatment of Drug Abuse: Toward a Balanced Perspective

Victor I. Friesen, MA

ABSTRACT. The role of the family in the etiology of drug abuse may be perceived in a significant proportion of adolescent and young adult substance abusers. This role is presented in the context of a systems and object-relations theory. A composite portrait of these generative types of families is presented in psychodynamic and affective terms, accompanied by guidelines and suggestions for family-based treatment.

INTRODUCTION

This paper focuses on the role of the family in the etiology and maintenance of substance abuse in one or more members. In recent years there has been a proliferation of articles and books on this subject, with emphasis on causation and treatment application and little in the way of limitations of applicability with many cases of drug abuse, or guidelines for selecting out these cases.[1,2] A few authors have actually advocated the necessity for family involvement in drug abuse treatment,[3] but the relative absence of a balanced perspective in the literature to date has inadvertently done a disservice to the field. It has, in effect, identified family therapy as a generally effective, broadband treatment modality for substance abusers, and this is clearly not the case. Specificity of treatment has long been recognized as an important factor in the progression of

Requests for reprints may be mailed to: Victor I. Friesen, MA, Philadelphia Psychiatric Center Drug Treatment Program, Ford Road and Monument Avenue, Philadelphia, Pennsylvania 19131, Telephone 215-581-3754.

© 1983 by The Haworth Press, Inc. All rights reserved.

77

psychotherapy in general,[4] and family therapy in particular.[5] There does appear to be a sub-population of substance abusers for whom family-oriented therapy may be viewed as a treatment of choice, and while it is not the purpose of this paper to postulate a cookbook for treatment, it may provide some rationale and basis for guidelines for family treatment applications with this population.

DRUG ABUSE AND THE FAMILY

There are various theories and causal explanations of substance abuse, including the biochemical, psychological and societal.[6] It seems, however, that the best working conception of an underlying basis or framework to drug abuse is to paraphrase the Humanist school of psychology: that people use drugs because drugs blunt bad feelings. For many millions of people the world is a crushingly complex, unhappy and lonely place, and for those who lack effective human solutions to this pain the use of drugs as one "solution" is surely not surprising. The ways and means through which this "solution" presents itself are often multi-determinant and interactive.[6] Writing in 1972, Brecher could state that with regard to the "causation" of substance abuse ". . . the vast bulk of evidence to date . . . favors the psychological and sociological theories. But this may be because the vast bulk of scientific studies throughout the past century has been devoted to a search for psychological and sociological factors."[6] Family therapy and research are fairly recent endeavors when compared with a century of drug abuse research, spanning only the past thirty years.[7] Within this period, however, there has been a vigorous growth in the search for family-based etiology of various pathological behaviors, including drug abuse.[8-11] In fact, over the past three decades the "family" (or lack of it) has been implicated in every major form of psychopathology, and these implications have even been extended into the areas of heart disease and cancer. When viewed in a social perspective as a procreative and cohabitive unit, the family is an important, but not necessarily primary, factor in the identity-forming and socialization process of a person,[12-14] and in the establishment of adaptive and maladaptive patterns in life.[13,15,16] Experiences gained outside the family can have profound effects on someone's life, particularly cohort experiences in formative years.[17,18]

The situation of searching for etiology patterns in the families of substance abusers is similar to the early research work on the families of schizophrenics. In 1965, Friedman[19] stated that while families of schizophrenics appear to be "different" from control families, there is no consistent evidence of a clear pattern to this difference in parents' personalities or interactions (and indeed, sometimes this difference has not been found at all). In brief, "No single factor, such as a faulty mother-infant relationship, seems likely to cause schizophrenia by itself but rather it seems to be the structure, milieu and interaction of the family that are detrimental to the ego development, the personality and the social adjustment of the children raised in them."[19] Recently Friedman[20] has indicated that results of research on the family in the development of psychopathology remain equivocal, suggesting that observed differences in family patterns are just a starting point in the search for etiology.

What then, can be said about the family of the substance abuser? Based on a review of seventeen articles on familial patterns in families with drug-abusing members, a fairly consistent pattern appears evident. Eight of these articles are based on survey research,[10,21-27] four are based on direct observation,[9,11,28,29] and five are themselves review articles of familial factors in substance abuse.[3,30-33] This review is not comprehensive, but represents a fair sampling of the literature on this area. With one exception[27] these articles describe family patterns significantly different from those of normal/control families. These patterns share several common elements and, while not fixed or absolute, have emphasized the following major aspects:

1. An emotionally conflicted relationship between parents of long standing.
2. An ineffectual and/or distant and inactive parent, often physically absent from the family. If present, s/he is minimally involved with the substance-abusing member on an emotional level except through negative affects.
3. A dominating and infantalizing parent, who is also emotionally immature, conflicted, and ambivalent about growth, individuation and separation in his/her children, particularly the drug abuser.
4. An emotionally disturbed and disturbing (by its very intensity), crisis-oriented feeling tone in the family which is both impacted and homeostatic, or balanced by the drug-abusing member.

5. Blurring and diffusion of cross-generational boundaries with the presence of pathological alliances between parents and children.

6. A family history of using and/or promoting the use of drugs as a method of coping with bad events and feelings.

A number of important considerations should be noted here. The first is that the majority of these survey and observational studies (the latter being distillations of therapists' impressions) are based on a rather narrow sampling range drawn from just those drug-abusers and their families most available for study. They are generally in the adolescent and young adult age range, and highly involved with one or more of their parents. Since this literature is heavily weighted on a younger age range and high family involvement, literature reviews also reflect this weighting, thus restricting the applicability of character descriptions, interactive patterns, and family dynamics in the etiology of substance abuse. It may be that the six family-based descriptors outlined above are applicable as important etiologic influences in the histories of older substance abusers, but it is difficult to apply them in cases of highly-fragmented family histories, or where the substance abuser has been raised in institutions, residential schools, or foster-homes.

Second, Binion,[27] in a very comprehensive survey of the family histories of 73 heroin-abusing women, found only subtle differences in the family backgrounds between comparative samples of women users and non-users. The most significant finding was the presence of more "blocked aspirations" for the user group. She concluded that drug abuse etiology is highly complex, and cannot be laid solely at the door of the family. Although limited to heroin-abusing subjects, this study may be a precursor to more finely-tuned surveys in this area.

Finally, Harbin and Mazier[31] and Cannon[10] have pointed out that the "drug abusing" family pattern is very similar to descriptions of families of schizophrenics, borderlines, narcissistic conditions and certain anti-social personality disorders. This suggests that various psychopathologies may share more in common in dysfunctional family patterns than has been hypothesized. This may be due to certain characterological/interactive features which become emergent when the family *is* involved, as part of a standard pattern. It would appear that there is no "unique" pattern to families of drug abusers, and that even a history of substance abuse in the family may prove to be a non-significant factor.

A Psychodynamic Portrait

Pattern "criteria" notwithstanding, descriptions of families of young drug abusers do convey very poignant impressions which can contribute to an important, treatment-oriented understanding of these families. In effect these descriptions offer a portrait of the family in psychological terms which can serve as a framework for dynamics and possible interventions. Reilly[11] has noted that drug abusing families often describe life as dull, lifeless and isolated from each other, with communication occurring primarily in negative ways through blaming, complaints, nagging, and correcting. Excitement becomes equated with crisis as acceptable behavior is ignored, and "bad" behavior is reinforced with attention and elevated involvement. Coupled with ambivalent parenting in the form of inconsistent limit-setting, denial of underlying frustration and unhappiness, unrealistically high or low expectations and pathological alliances and conflicts with the children, and a message of self-medication . . . "a young person will often turn to drugs, which serve a double function, for they not only allow one to spitefully revenge oneself upon demanding parents, but also provide a tailor-made excuse for every failure."[11]

Drug Abuse as a Family-System Solution

Given the dark aspect of anger and despair often seen in these families, and the pathological behaviors expressed, the question remains as to how might families "producing" a drug-abusing member get this way? The observations advanced so far suggest that since a familial "pattern" for drug abuse (where it does exist) may be more generalized than specific, certain working hypotheses from the family therapy literature appear useful in forming a working framework. These conceptualizations are presented at some length because of their implications for application in treatment.

Bell and Vogel,[34] in their work with schizophrenia, were among the first to suggest a generalized and applicable mechanism for the emergence of pathological behavior in a family child-member as the result of an intense loyalty and anxiety system. That is, the "scapegoat'' child is bound to the parental system through intense anxiety of abandonment and provides a crisis-ridden forum for the parents' marriage so they can avoid their own issues and conflict. This serves to preserve the marriage and the "life" of the child, since separation signals acute trauma, emotional abandonment, and death. Loyalty systems are many and varied, but Borzormenyi-Nagy and Spark[35] have outlined the fundamental aspects of how these systems can be engendered and enacted. One of the principal concepts in their writing has to do with the process of delegation. A delegate is one who fulfills a mission for the delegator and at the same time remains bound to his delegator, primarily through a sense of identification, obligation, and loyalty. The act of delegation can occur horizontally (maritally) and vertically (inter-generationally), although in general drug abuse appears to be part of a vertical delegation in drug abuse families.[9,11,36]

Friesen[36] has outlined the underlying dynamics of delegation in some detail. It is primarily the binding and separation-delaying affects of shame (personal failure before others) and its intertwined corollary guilt (transgressions against others) which are "disowned" by parents in the process of delegation. Shame/guilt binds play a major part in the drug abuser's family system. Briefly, the delegate takes on the burden of the delegator's shame or guilt through his or her own loyalty to the delegator by acting out failure and transgressions because they are too painful for the delegator. In a dysfunctional sense, massive delegation leads to an acting-out of the delegator's shame or guilt, resulting in a highly negative life pattern. The delegate becomes what the delegator has disowned, aiding in the delegator's denial of shame and projection of guilt. By living this out, the delegate can be easily shamed for disowned failure and made to feel guilty for disowned badness. However, by being so exploited and "cheated" of a healthy life, the delegate builds up an immense rage for the delegator, and is in a perfect position to operate the shame or guilt lever in return. That is, retaliation is achieved by living even more negatively since the delegator is bound to the delegate through the same mechanisms of identification and obligation which bind the delegate. In shame counter-delegation, the delegate confirms the delegator's shame-worthiness as a failed parent, and guilt-worthiness as a harmful and injurious parent who has hurt the delegate's development in life.[37] In families with massive delegation, these marital and intergenerational shame and guilt binds are cyclical and self-reinforcing, and become well-entrenched. A system is established which is extremely resistant to change, and is well-exemplified in families with drug abuse as a primary "symptom." This is a common course of adjustment for drug abusers and leads to a state of more or less chronic depression, a self-defeating life-style, suicidal ideation, and a number of masked suicides disguised as "accidents."

The Role of Unresolved Loss and Mourning

The family system of the young drug abuser is often conceptualized as balanced and homeostatic, with the drug abusing member as a necessary element. Reilly,[11] however, has related that this says nothing about *why* this system should arise at all. He suggests that the sources reside in the intergenerational histories of the parents, and that this history is generally one of impacted and impaired mourning or grief for profound emotional losses in their own families of origin. To this may be added the theme of unresolved anger toward those in the past who abandoned or rejected the parents in the family of the drug abuser. This anger is generally repressed and denied, but unconsciously acted out toward the delegated abuser as a form of retribution on the past, as the drug abuser is often a recreated bad object-relationship from the parents' own families of origin. Unresolved grief and mourning involve feelings and fears of rejection, abandonment, loss and death, and these feelings may be experienced long before the death of the parent-object has occurred. Briefly stated, these families appear to be impacted on death,[38,39] and while this is often masked by a layer of real concern for the drug abusing member, there is very often a strong "don't exist" message underlying this concern which is unconscious on the part of the parents (just as it may have been an unconscious message on the part of their own parents). They feel empty, and yet depressively tied to their "lost" love objects through a need to conserve the objects and also symbolically "punish" them through intropunitive rage. This depressive rage and pain is defended against by the projection of conflicts over loss and separation onto children. This creates the dull, lifeless, loveless, and negativistic atmosphere so common to substance abusing families. When a drug abusing member does die, tremendous guilt and shame/failure are induced in the parents. This guilt and shame are defended against through disownment of responsibility, the "blaming" of drugs, and the transformation of the dead member into an object of basic goodness who was irreparably flawed and just couldn't be "helped." Generally there is another delegate prepared for the role of the drug abuser.

CASE EXAMPLE

The family case example illustrates many of the above-outlined characteristics and dynamics which may be seen in the families of young drug abusers where involvement within the family is highly active. The "D" family consisted of the father, Bob (51), mother, Frances (51), a son, Bob Jr. (28), a daughter, Frances Ann (25), and a younger son, David (21). Both Bob Jr. and Frances Anne were married and living out of the parental home. David was unmarried and living at home.

The family came for treatment because of David's "drug problem." A drug overdose had precipitated his referral to the clinic by a family physician. At a deeper level it appeared that there had been a cumulative build-up toward a severe strain on the delicate balance of the family system, which had promoted and adjusted to his "problem" behavior (drugs, drug dealing, theft, etc.) over the past five years. His self-destructive behavior had accelerated faster than his family system could tolerate.

Socioeconomically, the family came from a lower middle class origin, with both parents being upwardly mobile. Bob had joined the police force when young and had risen to become a sergeant, while Frances had worked in the buying department of a clothing store chain for twenty years. Both Bob Jr. and Frances Anne had identified with their parents, as Bob Jr. worked as a policeman in the same precinct his father used to work in, while Frances Anne worked with her mother in the same buying department.

It is noteworthy, in light of the very strong loyalty themes in this family, that Bob was named for his father's father, who had been a hardworking, sober, responsible person all his life. In Bob's family of origin then, the intergenerational legacies and delegations could be traced back four generations, to David's great-grandfather. David was, in Bob's words, a "reincarnation" of his own father, who was an alcoholic, gambler, and numbers-runner all of his life. Named for his grandfather, David was the delegate for his father's anger toward his father, as well as the delegate for Bob's attempts to save his father through saving David. In saving David, Bob would be able to make reparation for his guilt for his anger toward his father, and failure to save him. Bob had done everything he could to win love, affection and acknowledgement from his father, even to nursing him when he was dying. He failed. The closest he'd come to being acknowledged was to be called the "best insurance going" by his father (in case he was caught running numbers, etc.), referring to his becoming a police sergeant. David's rise to prominence as a self-destructive behavior problem coincided with the time of Bob's father's death.

For his part, David got to act out the role of an irresponsible child in the family, being well cared for and eliciting a great deal of concern from his parents. He was also free to carry on his incestuously-based romance with mother. His love-hate relationship with her, as well as his suicidalness, was well exemplified by the fact that he had destroyed four of mother's cars in the past. She, on her part, kept lending them to him. Finally, David's behavior had served to maintain a focus for the parent's marriage, saving them from the responsibility of confronting any anger and hostility between each other.

The triangulated relationship of all three allowed the parents to continue expressing only loving concern for each other, as well as all of their children (including David). The children were also part of this, so that the whole emotional tone of the family was one of pseudomutuality, and avoidance of direct expression of negative feelings. By the time this family approached treatment their system, founded in past generational messages, was well-entrenched and resistant to change.

TREATMENT ASPECTS

Since adolescence is the phase of the life cycle during which the use of illicit drugs is usually initiated, and since adolescents are usually intensely involved in their relationships with their parents, it is natural to think of involving the family in the treatment of the adolescent drug abuser. Hirsch[40] was perhaps the first author, in the literature, who advocated family therapy as being appropriate for adolescent drug abuse. Typically, treatment for drug abuse has been applied within individual, group and residential modalities, separately and in various combinations. Family therapy is a relative newcomer to this therapeutic scene, but there is some supportive evidence for it. Based on their review of the few methodologically acceptable outcome studies available, Sowder et al[41] have concluded that this modality is at least as effective as other kinds of treatment. It is well to keep in mind, however, that the sample of studies serving as the basis for this conclusion is quite small (three in number), and that improvement in treatment may have more to do with longevity than modality applied. Sells[42] has indicated that for those substance abusers remaining in treatment for up to one year the improvement rate is approximately 70% to 80%, *regardless* of treatment modality entered. Tims[43] has stated that this improvement rate rises to roughly 90% after two years in any treatment modality.

Any practicing family therapist can attest to the special problems which seem to arise in maintaining families in therapy, since the forum for treatment appears to be more volatile than any other modality. One to two years of family treatment is a particularly long time, especially with adolescent and young adult drug-abusing members. This length of time does not appear to be essential, however, as it would seem that family therapy is more beneficial to the parents of the family initially, and this initial benefit can be used in separating the drug abuser from his or her enmeshed family system. There are few descriptions of the course of family therapy in drug treatment, but that provided by Stanton et al[2] of the structural approach would support this impression. It focuses on present-moment interactions in the family, realigning members, boundary-making and limit-setting, oriented toward healthy individuation and functioning. If the parents can be brought to look at their own lives, both in their families of origin and their current relationship, then the need for a delegate may be reduced. This may allow the younger members (even force them) to start working on their own lives.

Essentially then, the task of any family therapy approach in drug abuse derives from a systemic attitude common in all family therapy. The patient is the family, and the therapeutic work seems to revolve around a process of de-delegation while maintaining an impartial and empathic regard for all members. The family of the young drug-abuser, with high levels of family interaction and involvement, is particularly appropriate to family therapy intervention. Even though roles may be well-entrenched and resistant to change there is generally enough energy and real concern to harness in the therapeutic enterprise. If the parent-dyad can be strengthened through exploration and realignment of their relationship, then the systemic "need" for the drug abuser may be much decreased, but the process of de-delegation is, in reality, just a part of treatment. Patterns of drug abuse appear to be particularly resistant to change, and rather than confront the emotional pain of change, many continue to use drugs. Family therapy can initiate a freeing-up and emotional resolution process, but it is not a general panacea for delegated abusers. Individual and group therapy provide much-needed supports and forums for change for the person outside his or her "system." The responsibility for giving up drugs resides, ultimately, with the abuser. It is just this message of self-responsibility, embodied in a non-rescuing attitude and behavior in the therapists, which may prove to be the most helpful aspect of family treatment in the long run.[44] This message can serve as important role-modelling for members of the family caught up in a delegation and rescuing cycle.

CONCLUSIONS

There is some evidence to suggest an etiological connection between the family system and drug abuse, at least with younger, family-active abusers. The dynamics in these families are particularly interesting to clinicians and researchers in this area, but these dynamics may prove to be far less different from other pathological familial patterns, or even "normal" control families, than has been supposed. Certain formulations and hypotheses about "how" these families may work have proven useful in treatment, however, and by this fact alone deserve serious investigation.

It seems there is no one "type" of drug abuse, just as there is no one "type" of schizophrenia. The ways and means by which someone arrives at the abuse of drugs may eventually be traced differentially, according to dominant influencing factors (environment/peer, physiological, familial, etc.) and the absence of potentially counteractive factors (socioeconomic supports, role-models, supportive family systems, etc.). Treatment may become "path-designated" as a consequence, with certain treatment modalities being suggested as more appropriate than others for certain sub-populations. Family therapy seems to be most applicable to younger abusers with high levels of family involvement and family-based distress, and focusing on a process of de-delegation in the family. Of course family therapy is also applied with older substance abusers as parents in their own families, or as spouses in marital dyads, and is not just limited to families of younger abusers. These latter cases appear to present special problems to the practitioner in terms of exposure and "threat" to the abuser-client, however, and clinically may be less "appropriate" (because of therapy drop-outs) for family treatment.

At this point in time the verdict is far from in on family therapy, as there appears to be very little consistent data on how families may function, and even less on the actual process of treatment.[45] What is needed is more careful comparative research of family factors in the backgrounds of abusers and non-abusers, such as reported by Binion,[27] as well as careful observational studies of family interaction patterns and the testing of intervention strategies. This may help designate those situations in which the family is an important treatment factor, and how this treatment may be best approached.

REFERENCES

1. Kaufman E, Kaufmann PN, eds. Family therapy of drug and alcohol abuse. New York: Gardner Press, 1979.

2. Stanton MD, Todd TC, Associates. The family therapy of drug abuse and addiction. New York: The Guilford Press, 1982.

3. Davis DI, Klagsbrun M. Substance abuse and family interaction. Fam Proc 1977; 16: 149-64.

4. Garfield SL, Bergin AE, eds. Handbook of psychotherapy and behavior change: an empirical analysis. New York: John Wiley, 1978.

5. Gurman AS, Kniskern DP. Handbook of family therapy. New York: Brunner/Mazel, 1981.

6. Brecher EM. Licit and illicit drugs. Mount Vernon: Consumers Union, 1972.

7. Friesen VI. Family therapy and the historical moment. Fam Ther 1981;8:211-21.

8. Ferguson P, Lennox T, Lettieri DJ, eds. Drugs and family/peer influences. Washington: US Government Printing Office, 1974.

9. Kirschenbaum M, Leonoff G, Maliano A. Characteristic patterns in drug abuse families. Fam Ther 1974;1:43-62.

10. Cannon SR. Social functioning patterns in families of offspring receiving treatment for drug abuse. Roslyn Heights: Libra Publishing, 1976.

11. Reilly D. Drug abusing families: intrafamilial dynamics and brief triphasic treatment. In: Kaufman E, Kaufmann PN, eds. Family therapy of drug and alcohol abuse. New York: Gardner Press, 1979:115-30.

12. Lidz T. The family and human adaptation. New York: International Universities Press, 1963.

13. Block J. Lives through time. Berkeley: Bancroft Books, 1971.

14. Lidz T. The family and the development of the individual. In: Hofling CK, Lewis JM, eds. The family: evaluation and treatment. New York: Brunner/Mazel, 1980:45-70.

15. Vaillant G. Adaptation to life. Boston: Little, Brown, 1977.

16. Carter EA, McGoldrick M, eds. The family life cycle: a framework for family therapy. New York: Gardner Press, 1980.

17. Josephson E, Carroll EE, eds. Drug use: epidemiological and sociological approaches. New York: John Wiley, 1974.

18. Beschner GM, Friedman AS, eds. Youth drug abuse: problems, issues and treatment. Lexington: Lexington Books, 1979.

19. Friedman AS. The family and schizophrenia. In: Friedman AS, ed. Psychotherapy for the whole family. New York: Springer, 1965:15-19.

20. Friedman AS. Personal communication, 1982.

21. Wolk RL, Diskind MH. Personality dynamics of mothers and wives of drug addicts. Crime and Delinquency 1961;7:148-52.

22. Chein I, ed. The road to H: narcotics, delinquency, and social policy. New York: Basic Books, 1964.

23. Attardo N. Psychodynamic factors in the mother-child relationship in adolescent drug addiction: a comparison of mothers of schizophrenics and mothers of normal adolescent sons. Psychotherapy and Psychosomatics 1965;13:249-55.

24. Rosenberg CM. The young addict and his family. British J Psych 1971;118:469-70.

25. Blum RH, ed. Horatio Alger's children: the role of the family in the origin and prevention of drug risk. San Francisco: Jossey-Bass, 1972.

26. Haastrup S, Thomsen K. The social backgrounds of young addicts as elicited in interviews with their parents. Acta Psychiatrica Scandinavia 1972;48:146-73.

27. Binion VJ. A descriptive comparison of the families of origin of women heroin abusers and nonusers. In: Hall MB, ed. Addicted women: family dynamics, self-perceptions, and support systems. Washington: U.S. Government Printing Office, 1979:77-113.

28. Wellisch DK, Gay GR, McEntee R. The easy rider syndrome: a pattern of hetero-and-homosexual relationships in a heroin addict population. Fam Proc 1970;9:425-30.

29. Kaufman E, Kaufmann PN. From a psychodynamic orientation to a structural family therapy approach in the treatment of drug dependency. In: Kaufman E, Kaufmann PN, eds. Family therapy of drug and alcohol abuse. New York: Gardner Press, 1979:43-54.

30. Seldin NE. The family of the addict: a review of the literature. Int J Addictions 1972; 7:97-107.

31. Harbin HT, Mazier HM. The families of drug abusers: a literature review. Fam Proc 1975;14:411-31.

32. Green J. Overview of adolescent drug use. In: Beschner GM, Friedman AS, eds. Youth drug abuse: problems, issues and treatment. Lexington: Lexington Books, 1979: 17-44.

33. Stanton MD. Family treatment approaches to drug abuse problems: a review. Fam Proc 1979;18:251-80.

34. Bell NW, Vogel EF. The emotionally disturbed child as the family scapegoat. In: Bell NW, Vogel EF, eds. The family. Glencoe: Free Press, 1960:382-97.

35. Borzormenyi-Nagy I, Spark GM. Invisible loyalties. Hagerstown: Harper and Row, 1973.

36. Friesen VI. On shame and the family. Fam Ther 1979;6:39-58.

37. Stierlin H. Shame and guilt in family relations. Arch Gen Psych 1974;30:381-9.

38. Coleman SB. Incomplete mourning in the family trajectory: a circular journey to drug abuse. In: Ellis BG, ed. Drug abuse from the family perspective: coping is a family affair. Washington: U.S. Government Printing Office, 1980:18-31.

39. Stanton MD, Todd TC. Structural family therapy with drug addicts. In: Kaufman E, Kaufmann PN, eds. Family therapy of drug and alcohol abuse. New York: Gardner Press, 1979:55-9.

40. Hirsch R. Group therapy with parents of adolescent drug addicts. Psych Quart 1961; 35:702-10.

41. Sowder B, Dickey D, Glynn TJ. Family therapy: a summary of selected literature. Washington: U.S. Government Printing Office, 1979.

42. Sells SB. Treatment effectiveness. In: Dupont RL, Goldstein A, O'Donnell J, eds. Handbook on drug abuse. Washington: U.S. Government Printing Office, 1979:105-18.

43. Tims FM. Effectiveness of drug abuse treatment programs. Washington: U.S. Government Printing Office, 1981.

44. Friesen VI, Casella NT. The rescuing therapist: a duplication of the pathogenic family system. Am J Fam Ther 1982;10:57-61.

45. Pinsoff WM. Family therapy process research. In: Gurman AS, Kniskern DP, eds. Handbook of family therapy. New York: Brunner/Mazel, 1981:699-741.

Chronological Maturation
and Attempts at Deaddiction:
An Extension of the Maturation
Hypothesis

B. Krishna Singh, PhD
J. Sherwood Williams, PhD

ABSTRACT. This paper examines the relationship between chronological maturation and patterns of self-referrals to drug abuse treatment. The data used in the study were from the 1978 Client Oriented Data Acquisition Process distributed by the National Institute on Drug Abuse. Data on over 222,000 persons admitted to 1800 drug treatment centers throughout the United States were available from this source. The results of this analysis suggested that an attempt at deaddiction was positively related to the chronological maturation of the clients. These results were stable across race and sex. Some variations, however, were found depending on the primary type of substance for which the client was admitted to treatment.

Two prevailing views about addiction are that (1) once a person becomes an addict, s(he) remains an addict, i.e., "once an addict, always an addict," and (2) addicts "mature out of addiction" as they become older. Neither of these statements can be totally supported since there are those who do become deaddicted and there are those who remain addicted.[1] Winick[2] and Brill[3] note that pressures to become deaddicted loom larger as one becomes older. These

B. Krishna Singh is Director of Planning and Development, Richmond Public Schools, Richmond, VA 23219. J. Sherwood Williams is Director of the Virginia Commonwealth University Survey Research Laboratory and Associate Professor, Department of Sociology, Virginia Commonwealth University, Richmond, VA 23284. Reprint requests should be directed to Dr. Williams.

We appreciate the assistance provided by Alice C. Bryant and J. D. Cooper in the preparation of this manuscript.

© 1983 by The Haworth Press, Inc. All rights reserved.

91

pressures include a negative self-image, traumatic life events, repeated contacts with authorities and/or the fading glamour of drug use and may contribute to chronological maturation and deaddiction. Most of the above observations, however, have been based on the history of narcotic addiction and evidence on other types of substance abusers is unclear. Given the changing pattern of psychoactive substance use and abuse and thus, the changing composition of treatment populations, a reexamination of the process of chronological maturation and its role in the treatment seeking behavior and the process of deaddiction seems warranted.

The objective of this study is to examine how chronological maturation affects patterns of self-referrals to drug abuse treatment. Those who seek treatment on their own are presumably more motivated to become free of the addictive life-style as compared to those who enter treatment through legal or non-legal pressures. Self-referral is a choice made by the client although there may be external stimulus in seeking such treatment. Even so, these external factors are generally not as prominent for such clients as they are for other clients who enter treatment due to legal pressure (referral to treatment by social control agencies) or non-legal sources such as family, friends or others.

As noted earlier, the recent composition of treatment populations reflects changing patterns of drug misuse.[4-7] For example, the most recent patterns of treatment populations in the largest reporting system, i.e., Client Oriented Data Acquisition Process (CODAP), indicate only 45 percent of clients were admitted for heroin problems[7] as compared to 54.6 percent in 1977.[6] Comparing these percentages to the predecessor of CODAP, i.e., Drug Abuse Reporting Program (DARP), there were even higher proportions of heroin users in drug abuse treatment.[8]

This changing pattern of substance use and abuse and the changing composition of treatment population has significant implications for the deaddiction process. First, the physiological effects of the nonopiate drugs are considerably different from the narcotic drugs. Second, the legal implications of the use of nonopiate drugs are vastly different than the use of opioids, especially heroin. Third, assignment of immorality labels varies depending on the type of substance abuse or use as does the social stigma associated with a given type of substance abuse. For example, moderate use of alcohol is not only acceptable but is part of many social rituals while use of heroin is both strictly illegal and socially unacceptable. To some extent the use of marijuana apparently is becoming functionally equivalent to the use of alcohol.[10] Additionally, use of many addictive substances is not only legal but is heavily prescribed by physicians.

Given the varying implications of the type of drug problem for which clients may seek treatment on their own, it is expected that sex and race-ethnicity may have implications for the effect of chronological maturation on treatment seeking behavior. These expectations are based on the evidence that there are clear differences in sex-related patterns of substance abuse. For example, the use of psychotropic drugs is more frequent among women than men.[4,11] Race-ethnicity differences and the current trends indicate that there are disproportionately more blacks involved in the use of heroin than any other racial-ethnic group.[4-7]

The general hypothesis proposed is that regardless of the type of substance abuse or sex and racial grouping, the treatment seeking behavior becomes more prevalent as people become chronologically older. This does not imply that they will become deaddicted but only that treatment seeking behavior itself becomes more prevalent with chronological maturation.

METHOD

Data Source

The source of data for this study was the annual 1978 Client Oriented Data Acquisition Process (CODAP). The CODAP reporting system was a required reporting activity for all of the drug treatment and rehabilitation units receiving *any* federal support. In 1978 more than 1,800 units were reporting in the CODAP system, making it the largest single source of information on positively identified drug abusers in the nation.[12] The admissions to CODAP clinics represented nearly 60 percent of all admissions for drug abuse treatment in the nation.[7]

It should, however, be noted that the coverage of the CODAP system varied considerably from city to city and from state to state. Thus, while the overall national percentages are relatively high for known drug abusers who were in treatment for drug use and abuse in the CODAP clinics, the percentages would be less reflective if analyses were to be done at state or city levels. The extent to which CODAP clients differ from clients in other types of clinics is not known, although it is felt that clinics supported through state and local funds only will have approximately the same type of client composition. Those clinics which are supported through private sources only—which either charge clients or which accept funds from insurance sources—are likely to have clients who are generally older and have higher socio-economic status.[13]

In 1978, 222,634 clients were admitted to CODAP reporting clinics from whom 1978 CODAP admission forms were submitted. "Each admission reported in the CODAP data base does not necessarily represent a different client. For example, a client may be admitted to one clinic and then transferred to another clinic, which can provide appropriate treatment to that individual. To reduce multiple counting of such individuals, records of clients representing transfer admissions between CODAP clinics are not included.[5]

In this study, some further exclusions were made as noted below. First, clients admitted for primary drug problems other than the ten drug categories (heroin, other opiates, marijuana, barbiturates, amphetamines, alcohol, cocaine, hallucinogens, tranquilizers and other sedatives) were excluded. Second, those belonging to race-ethnic groups other than whites, blacks, and hispanics were also excluded. Because of these and other data exclusions by the CODAP report, this analysis uses approximately 97 percent of the 1978 CODAP clinic clients.

Dependent Measure

The dependent measure of this study is self-referral to treatment. This was determined by a self-reported measure by clients to persons filling out admission reports at the clinics. It should be noted that there are possible sources of errors in such a large reporting system such as lack of reporting, telescoping problems, incorrect entries and others. However, in a large reporting system such errors of classification and enumeration are unavoidable and there is no reason to suspect that these errors are not randomly distributed. Perhaps it should also be noted that "voluntary referrals" may have, in fact, contained a degree of either formal or informal coercion. Since we are limited to the data collected by CODAP we, unfortunately, have no way of determining the nature or degree of coercion that may have been directed at the clients.

Independent Measures

Three basic demographic measures were used in this study: These were sex (male-female), race (white, black and hispanic), and age (under 18, 18 to 20, 21 to 25, 26 to 30, and over 30). The primary drug problem at admission included ten categories. These were heroin, other opiates, marijuana, barbiturates, amphetamines, alcohol, cocaine, tranquilizers, hallucinogens, and other sedatives. The primary drug is "the drug type that is the major problem in that it has caused the most dysfunction. It is the drug problem for which the client was admitted to treatment. Only one primary problem may be reported."[7:307] Most clients, however, had secondary and tertiary drug usage, the most frequent of which were alcohol and marijuana.

Analysis

Since the sample sizes are very large in most categories of drugs, it is felt that almost all single and interactive effects would be significant. For this reason, the conventionally used methods for analyzing this type of data, such as loglinear analysis or weighed least square methods, were not used because of their insensitivity to extremely large samples, i.e., even trivial interactions have a tendency to become statistically significant.[14] In addition, since we have used the entire CODAP data set significance tests would be inappropriate. That is, we are working with a population at one point in time, not a sample. Thus, the analytical procedure is primarily inspection of percentages and percentage differences. In reporting the percentages, those cells that contained less than 20 cases are not reported since such percentages are not likely to be stable.[15]

RESULTS

The results data suggest that the type of primary drug problem was clearly related to the extent to which clients were likely to seek treatment voluntarily. Those clients who were addicted to opioids (including heroin) were much more likely to seek treatment on their own whereas marijuana clients were least likely to seek treatment on their own. One third of clients with alcohol and tranquilizer problems also came on their own to treatment. For the remainder of drug problems the proportion of self-referrals ranged between 28 to 30 percent. The differences between male and female clients, in terms of self-referral to treatment, did not appear to follow any consistent pattern. For example, based on the primary drug problems, more males than females came on their own if they had problems with other opiates and alcohol, whereas proportionately more females came on their own if they had marijuana, barbiturates, tranquilizers, and other sedatives problems. Generally, however, these differences were in the 4 to 7 percent range. The overall self-referral percentages were 39 percent and 39.4 percent for males and females respectively.

The patterns of self-referrals based on race-ethnicity generally indicated that blacks were most likely to seek treatment on their own than whites or hispanics. The largest difference was for alcohol using clients where blacks had 9 percent more self-referrals than whites and 7 percent more self-referrals than hispanics. Whites with hallucinogenic and tranquilizer problems were more likely to seek treatment than blacks or hispanics whereas hispanics with other opiate problems were more likely to seek treatment than were either white or black clients. The overall self-referrals were 34.8 percent for whites, 46.7 percent for blacks, and 41.6 percent for hispanic clients.

Perhaps the most interesting results appear in Table 1 showing patterns of self-referrals on the basis of age at admission in 1978. It was indicated that for each succeeding older age group, the proportion of clients who sought treatment on their own generally increased. For all drugs, the progressively higher proportions of clients in older age groups came to treatment on their own at least up to the 26-30 age group. This linear progression was evident through the over 30 age group for six drugs. Thus, the hypothesized trend appears to be supported; that is, as clients mature chronologically (which may mean a longer history of addiction), the effort to seek treatment on their own becomes more probable.

The extent to which there may be interactions among race-ethnicity, sex, and age in seeking treatment is examined in Table 2. It is seen that as clients became older, the percentages of self-referrals progressively increased regardless of race-ethnicity and sex grouping. The self-referrals increased for each older age category up to the 26-30 age category in most cases. In several categories of drugs the proportions of self-referrals were slightly higher for the 26-30 age group than for the over 30 age group. Generally, these differences were not more than 5 percent although some notable exceptions occurred. For example, among alcohol clients, the dif-

TABLE 1.   PERCENTAGES OF SELF-REFERRALS BY AGE AND TYPE OF PRIMARY
DRUG PROBLEM

Type of Primary Drug Problem	Age at Admission				
	< 18	18-20	21-25	26-30	> 30
Heroin					
%	19.5	37.1	48.7	52.9	53.7
n	405	4769	29083	36002	29378
Other Opiates					
%	12.8	33.8	49.3	56.9	52.1
n	265	1015	4626	4822	3708
Marijuana					
%	13.2	18.3	23.5	28.0	23.1
n	12699	6638	6785	2722	1555
Barbiturates					
%	14.8	24.9	30.7	36.3	37.9
n	1543	2012	3164	1781	1558
Amphetamines					
%	17.8	25.2	31.4	36.2	37.6
n	2026	2676	4158	2520	1848
Alcohol					
%	17.0	25.7	32.3	39.9	35.6
n	1375	1372	2773	3079	11657
Cocaine					
%	15.1	22.1	24.9	35.1	30.4
n	631	1163	1940	1287	839
Hallucinogens					
%	16.5	21.6	28.8	28.3	27.0
n	2721	3287	3806	1210	514
Tranquilizers					
%	14.6	24.1	33.5	38.4	39.8
n	874	796	1324	1084	2090
Other Sedatives					
%	14.6	23.1	29.4	38.5	41.9
n	835	866	1110	729	547

NOTE: Includes all clients regardless of racial-ethnic classification.   Only those clients are excluded whose drug problems were
other than those listed above.   This analysis is based upon approximately
97 percent of the clients.

ference between the two oldest groups (where proportions are contrary to what might be expected), white females and hispanic males,
was well over 10 percent apart. Similar patterns may be seen among
cocaine users for white females and for black males and females.
Another feature of interest was the 26-30 white female hallucinogen
cases whose self-referrals were closer to the under 18 age group. It
is also clear that black female tranquilizer users who were in the
18-20 age group had lower proportions of self-referral than the
under 18 age group.

SUMMARY AND DISCUSSION

The results of this study suggest that attempts at deaddiction
become more prevalent with chronological maturation. These attempts are apparently not influenced by the demographic classifica-

TABLE 2 .   PERCENTAGES OF SELF-REFERRALS BY PRIMARY DRUG PROBLEM AT
ADMISSION, RACE-ETHNICITY, SEX AND AGE

age by type of	White		Black		Hispanic	
primary drug problem	Male	Female	Male	Female	Male	Female
Heroin						
<18	26.0	13.8	12.3	33.3	17.9	26.2
18-20	33.6	38.0	33.1	42.0	38.2	39.5
21-25	45.7	47.9	51.2	50.8	46.6	50.5
26-30	52.1	50.7	54.3	54.9	50.8	49.4
>30	51.7	50.8	56.8	55.3	50.5	49.5
Other Opiates						
<18	9.1	18.9	10.7	15.4	a	a
18-20	32.7	35.5	32.0	17.2	17.2	13.3
21-25	47.5	47.5	49.4	50.3	50.3	54.7
26-30	54.6	51.8	61.3	50.0	50.0	59.6
>30	57.4	42.3	58.4	47.7	47.7	54.0
Marijuana						
<18	10.0	15.6	14.5	20.7	15.8	21.1
18-20	14.2	27.6	21.1	23.7	15.7	24.6
21-25	21.3	34.4	27.9	26.3	13.8	23.8
26-30	27.8	33.6	27.4	32.7	18.1	32.4
>30	28.7	37.9	23.0	33.3	19.1	a
Barbiturates						
<18	11.4	19.5	16.7	11.8	15.0	12.9
18-20	22.8	29.9	21.5	32.8	21.3	37.1
21-25	28.9	36.3	29.8	29.3	30.8	17.5
26-30	36.3	40.1	34.2	30.0	30.5	38.9
>30	40.2	40.6	33.5	23.6	33.8	32.0
Amphetamines						
<18	16.2	18.0	30.1	17.4	11.1	17.9
18-20	21.6	29.7	36.1	30.8	19.3	15.3
21-25	28.2	34.5	42.9	20.0	24.8	32.1
26-30	33.5	35.4	48.5	31.1	20.0	a
>30	36.6	37.6	44.4	38.7	27.1	a
Alcohol						
<18	14.9	16.4	17.4	31.6	21.2	21.7
18-20	21.1	32.4	32.5	46.2	25.7	a
21-25	30.1	28.2	40.7	44.0	32.2	33.0
26-30	38.1	39.0	44.9	38.7	50.0	30.0
>30	35.8	27.8	43.4	37.3	33.3	41.7
Cocaine						
<18	10.9	18.8	15.7	19.2	22.2	18.2
18-20	21.0	24.6	24.9	16.5	27.8	10.7
21-25	28.6	29.3	34.1	33.3	22.1	28.1
26-30	32.7	41.4	36.9	40.8	25.8	a
>30	31.6	27.8	30.8	28.6	27.6	a
Hallucinogens						
<18	13.3	19.1	16.3	22.2	17.6	30.9
18-20	21.5	28.8	16.9	21.0	17.1	18.8
21-25	27.2	33.8	17.2	19.9	19.9	17.8
26-30	34.7	20.5	19.5	16.7	26.3	27.7
>30	31.3	46.2	15.3	18.5	21.1	a
Tranquilizers						
<18	11.8	18.4	9.1	24.3	4.0	a
18-20	20.9	33.6	20.6	5.9	32.3	a
21-25	31.5	37.7	26.9	24.4	46.4	17.4
26-30	35.4	39.3	39.6	44.4	42.9	a
>30	46.8	39.3	32.6	36.8	a	a
Other Sedatives						
<18	13.7	18.4	7.7	7.5	a	a
18-20	17.6	32.8	38.6	19.4	16.7	a
21-25	26.9	33.9	31.6	31.6	27.7	a
26-30	35.4	39.3	39.6	44.4	42.9	a
>30	46.8	39.3	32.6	36.8	a	a

a= less than 20 cases in the cell; not stable for computations of
proportions.   For number of clients, see other tables.   This analysis
is based upon approximately 92 percent of the clients.

tion of sex, although there are some differences based on race-ethnic groupings. However, the type of substance abuse at admission does determine the extent to which clients will seek treatment on their own. The present analysis finds that while opiate users are most likely to seek treatment on their own, marijuana users are least likely to do so. The differential rates of self-referrals based on substance abuse are indicative of differential debilitating effects as well as perceived harmfulness of different types of substances. It should be noted, however, that regardless of the type of substance abuse, the most relevant factor for self-referral appears to be chronological maturation.

Attempts at deaddiction, with chronological maturation, may be more prevalent for several reasons. First, as one gets older, the rebelliousness, which may have contributed to initial and continuing drug use during the individual's younger years, tends to subside. Second, the peer group influence (which has consistently been found to influence drug use) tends to become scattered and the support for continuing drug use diminishes. Third, continuing problems with social control agencies, life events and other traumatic factors may provide a major impetus for seeking treatment as one gets older.[2,3]

The clinical implications of self-referral to treatment can be foreseen in several ways. First, clients who seek treatment on their own are more highly motivated to become deaddicted. The challenge for treatment programs is to capitalize on such motivations. Second, programs serving chronologically mature clients should be designed to follow a treatment approach which best serves their needs. As it currently appears, the majority of treatment programs are oriented toward treating younger clients and this is especially true of outpatient drug free programs. The treatment programs would need major modifications relative to their philosophy, treatment process, and services provided in order for them to effectively deal with their mature clients. Third, treatment programs dealing with younger clients have a more difficult task and this factor must be considered when resources are allocated.

While the data suggest that chronological maturation is clearly a very important factor in treatment seeking behavior, it must be added that the present study is not a direct test of the maturation hypothesis as proposed by Winick.[2] It does, however, suggest that along with chronological maturation, self-attempts to become deaddicted become more common. At the same time, it also suggests that the type of substance abuse is important in designing treatments.

Given the changing composition of treatment populations (at least in federally funded treatment programs), it becomes imperative that the focus of treatment not be solely on treatment of opiates and the models of treating heroin addicts should not be imposed in treating clients whose primary drug problems are nonopiate drugs.

It has been argued in this paper that self-referral to treatment is an indicator of high motivation on the part of clients to become deaddicted. While the measurement of motivation to seek treatment on one's own can become a major point of contention in the measurement of motivation, the evidence from other studies suggests that clients who come to treatment on their own are more likely to do better in treatment.[16-20]

To what extent the chronological maturation itself may be more relevant than self-referral cannot be clearly determined in the present study. However, it is logical to assume that chronological maturation affects motivation to seek treatment since motivation to seek treatment can hardly be expected to affect chronological maturation. Thus, the causal sequence best suited for the present study is one which considers chronological maturation as one of the major factors in treatment seeking behavior.

It should be clearly noted that while chronological maturation may give an impetus to seek treatment, the success and failure in treatment is dependent upon a number of other factors which are above and beyond the relationship between chronological maturation and treatment behavior. For example, background factors, treatment process variables, the type and intensity of treatment received are better predictors of success or failure in treatment. Chronological maturation simply suggests that as people get older they are more likely to seek assistance from treatment agencies which may help their retreat from an addictive life-style.

REFERENCES

1. Vaillant GE. The natural history of narcotic drug addiction. Seminars in Psychiatry. 1970;b:486-8.

2. Winick C. The life cycle of the narcotic addict and of addiction. Bulletin of Narcotics. 1964;16:1-11.

3. Brill H. The process of deaddiction. New York: The Free Press, 1972.

4. Cisin I, Miller JD, Harrell AV. Highlights from the National Survey on Drug Use. Washington, D.C.: Civil Printing Press, 1977.

5. National Institute on Drug Abuse. Annual Data, 1976. Series E. Rockville, MD: NIDA, 1977.

6. National Institute on Drug Abuse Annual Data, 1977. Series E. Rockville, MD: NIDA, 1978.

7. National Institute on Drug Abuse. NDATUS, Series E. Rockville, MD: NIDA, 1978.

8. Simpson DD, Savage LJ, Lloyd MR, Sells SB. Evaluation of drug treatment. Washington, D.C.: Government Printing Press, 1978.

9. Duster T. The Legislation of Morality. New York: The Free Press, 1970.

10. Singh BK, Knezek L, and Adams LD. Changes in reactions to deviance: The issue of legalization of marijuana. Journal of Drug Issues, 1979;9:499-10.

11. Abelson H, Fishburne P. Psychoactive Substance Abuse Survey. Rockville, MD: NIDA, 1976.

12. National Institute on Drug Abuse. Annual Data, 1978, Series E. Rockville, MD: NIDA, 1979.

13. Singh BK, Joe GW. Substance abuse and arrests: Variations in pre-treatment arrests of clients in drug treatment programs. Criminology 1981;19:315-27.

14. Reynolds HT. The Analysis of cross-classifications. New York: The Free Press, 1977.

15. Steele L, Torrie E. Principles of Statistics. New York: The Free Press, 1960.

16. Gendreau P, Grendeau LP. Research design and narcotic addiction process. Canadian Psychiatric Association Journal, 1971;16:265-7.

17. Paynard C, Wolf KW, Dreachslin J. Source of referral as an indicator of motivational factors and treatment outcome with drug dependent clients. The International Journal of the Addictions, 1979;14:645-56.

18. Penk WE, Robinowitz A. Personality differences of volunteer and non-volunteer heroin and nonheroin drug abusers." Journal of Abnormal Psychology, 1978;85:91-0.

19. Penk WE, Robinowitz A. A test of voluntarism hypothesis among nonvolunteering opiate addicts who voluntarily return to treatment. Journal of Abnormal Psychology, 1980; 89:234-9.

20. Singh BK, Joe GW, Sells SB, Cole EC. Behavioral outcomes of clients in drug treatment. Fort Worth, TX, Institute of Behavioral Research, 1980.

Selective Guide to Current Reference Sources on Topics Discussed in this Issue

Mary Mylenki, MSLS

Each issue of *Advances in Alcohol and Substance Abuse* features a section offering suggestions on where to look for further information on that issue's theme. Our intent is to guide readers to sources which will provide substantial information on the specific theme presented, rather than on the entire field of alcohol and substance abuse. We aim to be selective, not comprehensive, and in most cases we shall emphasize current rather than retrospective material.

Some reference sources utilize designated terminology (controlled vocabularies) which must be used to find material on topics of interest. For these a sample of available search terms is indicated to enable the reader to assess the suitability of each source for his/her purposes. Other reference tools use key words or free text terms (generally from the title of the document, agency or meeting listed). In searching the latter the user should look under all synonyms for the concept in question.

Readers are encouraged to consult with their librarians for further assistance before undertaking research on a topic.

Suggestions regarding the content and organization of this section are welcomed.

1a. INDEXING AND ABSTRACTING TOOLS

Biological Abstracts. Philadelphia, BioSciences Information Service, 1926– , semi monthly.
   Keyword subject index, e.g., addiction; depression; narcotic(s).

Mary Mylenki is Senior Assistant Librarian, Payne Whitney Psychiatric Clinic Library, New York Hospital-Cornell Medical Center, New York, NY.

© 1983 by The Haworth Press, Inc. All rights reserved.

103

Dissertation Abstracts International. A. Humanities and Social Science. B. Sciences and Engineering. Ann Arbor, MI, University Microfilms International, 1938–   , monthly.
  Keyword title index.
Chicago Psychoanalytic Literature Index. Chicago, IL, Institute for Psychoanalysis, 1920–   , quarterly.
  Search terms: Alcohol; alcoholism; alcoholics anonymous; addiction; addiction, drug; drug abuse; adolescence; adolescents; family; family therapy; depression; sex and sexuality; sociopathic personality.
Excerpta Medica: Psychiatry. Section 32. Amsterdam, The Netherlands, Excerpta Medica, monthly.
  Search terms: Alcohol; alcoholism; alcoholics anonymous; depression; drug abuse; drug dehabituation; drug dependence; narcotic dependence; opiate addiction; family; family psychiatry; sexual dysfunction; sociopathy.
Excerpta Medica: Drug Dependence. Section 40. Amsterdam, The Netherlands, Excerpta Medica, monthly.
  Search terms: Alcohol; alcoholism; alcohol withdrawal syndrome; depression; drug abuse; family; family therapy.
Hospital Literature Index. Chicago, IL, American Hospital Association, 1955–   , quarterly.
  Indexed as is *Index Medicus* (see below). Covers literature related to administration, planning and financing of health care facilities; does not cover clinical aspects of patient care.
Index Medicus (including Bibliography of Medical Reviews). Bethesda, MD, National Library of Medicine, 1960–   , monthly.
  Controlled vocabulary MeSH terms. See: Alcoholism; alcohol deterrents; alcohol withdrawal delirium; alcoholics anonymous; antisocial personality; depression; depressive disorder; adolescence; family; family therapy; narcotics; narcotic dependence; poverty areas; sex disorders; skid row alcoholics; substance abuse; substance dependence. Coordinate these terms and/or use subheading "psychology."
Inventory of Marriage and Family Literature. Minneapolis, MN, Family Social Science Department, University of Minnesota, 1967–   ; annual as of 1980, vol. 6. Covers literature from 1900.
  Indexed by keywords in titles and a limited broad subject index.
Psychological Abstracts. Arlington, VA, American Psychological Association, 1927–   , monthly.
  Search terms: Alcohol drinking patterns; alcohol intoxication;

alcohol rehabilitation; alcoholics anonymous; alcoholism; antisocial behavior; antisocial personality; depression (emotion); drug abuse; drug dependence; family crises; family relations; family therapy; ghettoes; problem drinking; sexual function disturbances; social drinking.

Social Science Citation Index. Science Citation Index. Philadelphia, PA, Institute for Scientific Information, 1961–   , bimonthly.

See: *Permuterm Subject Index,* e.g., alcohol, depression, family. May also be searched through *Citation Index* by known authors in the area of interest.

1b. ON-LINE BIBLIOGRAPHIC DATA BASES

BIOSIS (*Biological Abstracts* citations).

Search as in printed index and title keywords.

EXCERPTA MEDICA

Guide to the Excerpta Medica Classification System is available. Search as in printed index.

MEDLINE (Medical Literature Analysis and Retrieval System On-line)

Index Medicus citations using MeSH search terms.

PsycINFO (Psychological Abstracts)

In addition to Psychological Abstracts thesaurus may use free text terms, search both titles and abstracts.

1c. CURRENT AWARENESS PUBLICATIONS

Current Contents: Social and Behavioral Sciences. Philadelphia, Institute for Scientific Information, 1968–   , weekly.

Title word index.

Journal of Studies on Alcohol. Bi-monthly current literature issues; specific subject index.

Search terms: Addiction-alcohol; addiction-drugs; depressions; family therapy-alcoholism. Use ''alcoholism'' as a subheading with many subjects, e.g., family; sex.

2. BOOKS

Current Catalog. Bethesda, MD, National Library of Medicine, 1966–   , quarterly.

Search terms same as *Index Medicus* (MeSH).

Chicorel Index to Mental Health Book Reviews. New York, American Library Publishing Co., annual.
  Search terms: Alcoholism and drug abuse; depression; family therapy.

3. U.S. GOVERNMENT PUBLICATIONS

Monthly Catalog of United States Government Publications. Washington, DC, U.S. Government Printing Office, monthly.
  Search terms: Alcoholism; depression, mental; narcotic habit-treatment.

4. SOURCES OF INFORMATION ON GRANTS

Annual Register of Grant Support. Chicago, Marquis Academic Media, annual.
  Indexed by subject, agencies, programs, geographic areas.
Foundation Grants Index. New York, Foundation Center, annual.
  Indexed by subject.

5. JOURNAL LISTINGS

Ulrich's International Periodicals Directory. 20th ed. New York, R. R. Bowker Co., 1981.
  Broad subject index.

6. GUIDE TO UPCOMING MEETINGS

World Meetings: Medicine. New York, Macmillan Publishing Co., quarterly.
  Keyword subject index, directory of sponsors.
Guide to Psychiatry Meetings. Woodbury, NY, Publishing, Representation and Research, Inc., 1982, 3/year.
  Lists both national and international meetings chronologically.

7. PROCEEDINGS OF MEETINGS

Conference Papers Index. Louisville, KY, Data Courier, Inc., 1973– , monthly.
Index to Scientific and Technical Proceedings. Philadelphia, Institute for Scientific Information, monthly.

Keyword subject index similar to other ISI publications, and other indexes including sponsors.

InterDok Directory of Published Proceedings. White Plains, NY, InterDok Corp., 1965– , 10/year, annual cumulation.
Keyword by conference name and by title; sponsor index.

8. SPECIAL LIBRARY COLLECTIONS

Ash, L., comp. *Subject Collections,* 5th ed. New York, R. R. Bowker Co., 1978.
Search terms: alcohol; alcoholism; community mental health services; drug habit; drugs; mental hygiene.

Lenroot-Ernst, L., ed. *Directory of Special Libraries and Information Centers. Vol. 3. Health Sciences Libraries,* 7th ed. Detroit, Gale Research Co., 1982.
Search headings: Alcohol & alcoholism; drug abuse, mental health.

Information for Authors

Advances in Alcohol & Substance Abuse publishes original articles and topical review articles related to all areas of substance abuse. Each publication will be issue-oriented and may contain both basic science and clinical papers.

All submitted manuscripts are read by the editors. Many manuscripts may be further reviewed by consultants. Comments from reviewers will be returned with the rejected manuscripts when it is believed that this may be helpful to the author(s).

The content of *Advances in Alcohol & Substance Abuse* is protected by copyright. Manuscripts are accepted for consideration with the understanding that their contents, all or in part, have not been published elsewhere and will not be published elsewhere except in abstract form or with the express consent of the editor. Author(s) of accepted manuscripts will receive a form to sign for transfer of author's(s') copyright.

The editor reserves the right to make those revisions necessary to achieve maximum clarity and conciseness as well as uniformity to style. *Advances in Alcohol & Substance Abuse* accepts no responsibility for statements made by contributing author(s).

MANUSCRIPT PREPARATION

A double-spaced original and two copies (including references, legends, and footnotes) should be submitted. The manuscript should have margins of at least 4 cm, with subheadings used at appropriate intervals to aid in presentation. There is no definite limitation on length, although a range of fifteen to twenty typed pages is desired.

A cover letter should accompany the manuscript containing the name, address, and phone number of the individual who will be specifically responsible for correspondence.

Title Page

The first page should include title, subtitle (if any), first name, and last name of each author, with the highest academic degree obtained. Each author's academic and program affiliation(s) should be noted, including the name of the department(s) and institution(s) to which the work should be attributed; disclaimers (if any); and the name and address of the author to whom reprint requests should be addressed. Any acknowledgements of financial support should also be listed.

Abstracts

The second page should contain an abstract of not more than 150 words.

References

References should be typed double space on separate pages and arranged according to their order in the text. In the text the references should be in superscript arabic numerals. The form of references should conform to the Index Medicus (National Library of Medicine) style. Sample references are illustrated below:

1. Brown MJ, Salmon D, Rendell M. Clonidine hallucinations. Ann Intern Med. 1980; 93:456–7.
2. Friedman HJ, Lester D. A critical review of progress towards an animal model of alcoholism. In: Blum K, ed. Alcohol and opiates: neurochemical and behavioral mechanisms. New York: Academic Press, 1977:1–19.
3. Berne E. Principles of group treatment. New York: Oxford University Press, 1966.

Reference to articles in press must state name of journal and, if possible, volume and year. References to unpublished material should be so indicated in parentheses in the text.

It is the responsibility of the author(s) to check references against the original source for accuracy both in manuscript and in galley proofs.

Tables and Figures

Tables and figures should be unquestionably clear so that their meaning is understandable without the text. Tables should be typed double space on separate sheets with number and title. Symbols for units should be confined to column headings. Internal, horizontal, and vertical lines may be omitted. The following footnote symbols should be used: * † ‡ § ¶

Figures should be submitted as glossy print photos, untrimmed and unmounted. The label pasted on the back of each illustration should contain the name(s) of author(s) and figure number, with top of figure being so indicated. Photomicrographs should have internal scale markers, with the original magnification as well as stain being used noted. If figures are of patients, the identities should be masked or a copy of permission for publication included. If the figure has been previously published, permission must be obtained from the previous author(s) and copyright holder(s). Color illustrations cannot be published.

Manuscripts and other communications should be addressed to:

Barry Stimmel, MD
Mount Sinai School of Medicine
One Gustave L. Levy Place
Annenberg 5-12
New York, New York 10029

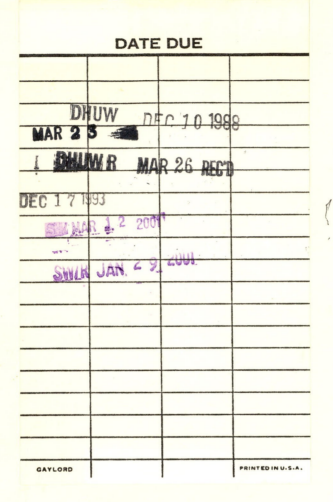

DATE DUE

	DHUW	DEC 10 1988	
MAR 2 3			
DHUW R	MAR 26 REC'D		
DEC 17 1993			
MAR 12 2001			
SWLR JAN 2 9 2001			
GAYLORD			PRINTED IN U.S.A.

GAYLORD   PRINTED IN U.S.A.